TODAY'S
TENTMAKERS

D0194249

TODAY'S
TENTMAKING

TODAY'S TENTMAKERS

Self-support—
An alternative model
for worldwide witness
J. Christy Wilson, Jr.

Overseas Counseling Service
a division of CRISTA
Box 33836
Seattle, WA 98133
(206) 546-7555

Deep gratitude is expressed to my wife Betty, who has been an ever loving partner, to Jim and Margaret Cudney and all the trustees of the Kabul Community Church for all their help and encouragement, and to Holly Greening for her faithful secretarial work. Thanks are also extended to the trustees and administrators of Gordon-Conwell Theological Seminary for the half-year sabbatical which made this book possible, and to Ken and Margaret Taylor, Wendell Hawley, Virginia Muir, Ken Petersen, and other friends at Tyndale House.

All Scripture quotations are taken from the King James Version of the Bible unless otherwise noted. Other translations and paraphrases used include: *The Living Bible* (TLB), the *New International Version* (NIV), and the *New American Standard Bible* (NASB).

Library of Congress Catalog Card Number 79-90737
ISBN 0-8423-7279-2
Copyright © 1979 by J. Christy Wilson, Jr.
All rights reserved
Published in the United States of America
Tyndale House Publishers, Inc.
Wheaton, Illinois

To the Lord Jesus Christ
who was himself a self-supporting carpenter,
and to all other tentmakers
serving around the world today

CONTENTS

FOREWORD

As a pastor for forty years, I led a church which supported 142 missionaries at a cost of $250,000 a year. Today, that same church supports seventy-two missionaries and spends $510,000, or $7,000 per person. How many local congregations can maintain a missionary enthusiasm when the sending of a missionary couple to Latin America, India, or Europe costs more than the congregation pays its own pastor? Missionaries are needed, but local costs are skyrocketing.

Today's Tentmakers is the answer to the inflationary costs of missions. I believe Dr. Wilson has uncovered the biblical answer to our problems. He advocates missionary self-support, just as Paul supported himself by tentmaking.

Many people are going abroad to take responsible jobs for companies or to teach under the pay of foreign governments. Why can't these people, financially supported by their own vocation, be missionaries too? Certainly dangers exist—these are outlined here by Dr. Wilson. But dedication to Christ and evangelism can counteract these difficulties. A new understanding of these opportunities and a clarity of purpose will open many doors for unofficial missionary endeavor.

Dr. Wilson tells of the great example of Henry Martyn (a tentmaking missionary), shows how the Muslims are spreading their faith through lay evangelism, and emphasizes those organizations which are giving themselves to tentmaking activity today. God is challenging young people to world outreach with the gospel. Means of fulfilling this call are open. Dedication to tentmaking may be the way of answering the call.

Harold J. Ockenga
President Emeritus
Gordon-Conwell Theological Seminary

PREFACE

The purpose of this book is to inspire, inform, encourage, and challenge those whom God is calling to serve as his tentmakers, his self-supporting witnesses around the world. It also seeks to acquaint the Church with the unprecedented opportunity Christian lay people have of engaging in their professions abroad while at the same time being ambassadors for Christ. As the Holy Spirit in Acts opened the door of faith to the Gentiles even before the early Church considered it, so today potential self-supporting Christian missionaries are all around the world while many are not yet aware of what has happened. With mainland China, Russia, and many Muslim nations opening more and more to this type of witness, may we today have ears to hear what the Spirit is saying to the churches.

Finally, this work seeks to make all Christians aware of their responsibility to pray for, assist, and encourage self-supporting witnesses along with regular missionaries in order that the good news of Jesus Christ may be taken to every person in our generation. In this way we can help fulfill what our Lord told us to pray daily, "Thy kingdom come. Thy will be done in earth, as it is in heaven."

1/AN EXCITING OPENING

God . . . is able to do far more than we would ever dare to ask or even dream of (Eph. 3:20, TLB).

There was a spirit of excitement. Ralph Winter had walked into the Inter-Varsity headquarters office on Chicago's Lake Street early in 1947. Shortly before this he, along with David Howard, Jim Elliot, and others, had attended the student Missionary Convention, later to become known as "Urbana" but which was first held at the University of Toronto. The theme of this conference had been "Completing Christ's Commission." Dr. Harold Ockenga, Brother Bakht Singh, and Dr. Samuel Zwemer had challenged those there with reaching the unreached people of the world with the gospel. One nation which was still closed was Afghanistan in Central Asia. Missionaries had worked and prayed on the borders for almost a hundred years. Yet permission to work in that country had been continually denied. It was completely unevangelized, without one Afghan Christian, although it was a nation geographically larger than France. But now a student had spotted a notice posted on the bulletin board at Columbia Teachers College in New York stating that teachers were wanted in Afghanistan!

Ralph Winter had come to pray and to plan with those of us in the Chicago office about the best way to bring this opportunity before qualified Christians across the United States and Canada so that they could apply for these positions. The government of Afghanistan offered to pay a small salary plus transportation for teachers who were qualified. Even though missionaries were not allowed in that land, "tentmakers" were wanted.

Ken Taylor, editor of *His* magazine, agreed to run a feature article in one issue along with a cover highlighting this opportunity by depicting a camel caravan going through the Khyber Pass into Afghanistan.

Stacey Woods, who was general secretary, authorized the sending of this information to the chapters on secular campuses as well as to the Student Foreign Missions Fellowship groups in Christian colleges, Bible schools, and seminaries throughout North America. Since I was missionary secretary, he gave this responsibility to me.

Miss Margaret Haines of Philadelphia had been a missionary on the border of Afghanistan. After she was forced to return to the States because of health, she edited and distributed a news and prayer bulletin entitled "Missions on the Borders of Afghanistan." As a member of the Board of Inter-Varsity, she had also attended the Toronto Student Convention. After we contacted her about this new opportunity for teachers to go to Afghanistan, she agreed to send detailed information to any who were interested.

Thus the plan providentially took shape to recruit a team of Christian teachers who could go into Afghanistan as "tentmakers." The spirit of excitement that day came from the realization that God might be calling us to be his instruments to secure entrance for the good news about Jesus Christ in the closed land of Afghanistan. Had not our Lord promised, "This gospel of the kingdom shall be preached in all the world for a witness unto all nations"?

But little did we realize that this would develop into a whole new model for missions.

2/AN UNPRECEDENTED OPPORTUNITY

*What wonderful things God has ready for those who love the Lord.
. . .We know about these things because God has sent his Spirit to
tell us* (1 Cor. 2:9, 10, TLB).

Little did those working on the Afghanistan project realize that
through this God was planning the way self-supporting witnesses
could be used to extend his gospel to closed countries around the
world. The greatest privilege for any Christian is to participate in
the completing of Christ's Commission at home and abroad.
Self-supporting witness affords this opportunity for many.

Dr. Waldron Scott, general secretary of the World Evangelical
Fellowship, recently commented about tentmaking service: "I feel
in my soul that this perhaps is the next great creative movement
that God's Spirit is going to bring into existence in missionary
efforts . . . . We are talking about a project that is at least as big
in size as the total missionary movement today and maybe much
bigger."[1]

Dr. Kane of Trinity observes, "Today there are millions of
Americans traveling and residing overseas. If all the dedicated
Christians among them could be trained and persuaded to be
effective witnesses for Jesus Christ, they would add a whole new
dimension to the missionary movement. The spiritual potential
here is enormous."[2] He also affirms, "This is the wave of the
future."

The late Canon Max Warren wrote, "I believe there is a call for
an entirely new type of missionary activity to be developed

alongside the traditional modes . . . . Men and women . . . going
. . . as ordinary salaried officials . . . to work . . . in light of
Christian insights. Promotion and financial reward will be
completely subordinated to their Christian vocation."[3]

But how does such a person and vocation differ from that of
one whom we traditionally know as a missionary? Roland Allen
defines a missionary as a person "who is called by God to
communicate to others the secret life of Jesus."[4] Also, the meaning
coming from the etymology of the Latin word *mitto,* which is the
verb "to send," signifies that a missionary is "one who is sent."
The similar Greek word is *apostello,* from which we get the word
"apostle" or "one who is sent." Thus a missionary is a person
who is sent by Jesus Christ. He states this idea in his Commission:
"As my Father hath sent me, even so send I you" (John 20:21).

But what is the reason behind his Commission? He answers this
by explaining that "repentance and remission of sins should be
preached in his name among all nations" (Luke 24:47). Or again,
our Lord ordered, "Go into all the world, and preach the gospel
to every creature" (Mark 16:15). But what is this message which
the sent ones are to proclaim? The Apostle Paul defines it: "The
gospel . . . is . . . that Christ died for our sins just as the
Scriptures said he would, and that he was buried, and that three
days afterwards he arose from the grave" (1 Cor. 15:1–4, TLB).

In a real sense, every Christian is a witness to this life-changing
message that "God so loved the world, that he gave his only
begotten Son, that whosoever believeth in him should not perish,
but have everlasting life." Every Christian can be called a "sent
one" or apostle in the sense of being a witness, as the psalmist
exhorts: "Let the redeemed of the Lord say so."

But there is also a specialized meaning for "missionary" which
refers to a person who is a cross-cultural witness. Our Lord told
his disciples, "When the Holy Spirit has come upon you, you will
receive power to testify about me with great effect, to the people
in Jerusalem, throughout Judea, in Samaria, and to the ends of
the earth" (Acts 1:8, TLB). For the disciples to be able to witness
in Samaria and to the ends of the earth, this needed to be done
cross-culturally, since people in these areas had different customs,
thought forms, or languages. Thus, the technical meaning of
"missionary" is a person who has been sent to witness to those of
another culture. Our Lord's Great Commission states that we are
to make disciples from among all nations or ethnic groups.[5] This
therefore assumes that cross-cultural witness will be carried out.

The Holy Spirit further emphasized this when he gave the disciples at Pentecost the supernatural power to witness in the different languages of the people who were gathered in Jerusalem.

But the Scriptures say that there are two types of cross-cultural witnesses. The first are those who receive full support from churches. This is the way the Apostle Peter was supported. On the other hand, the Apostle Paul earned his own salary by making tents. Even today, cross-cultural witnesses or "missionaries" fall into these two categories. Some are funded by the contributions of fellow Christians, while others support themselves through various professions.

Different terms have been used to define and characterize "tentmakers." Since this is a new concept to many, it has been difficult to settle on an expression in our vocabulary that signifies what is really meant. Some have referred to them as "non-professional missionaries."[6] Arthur Glasser and Eric Fife have rightfully noted that this terminology is not without problems. It, on the one hand, refers to a regular missionary as a "professional," which carries a connotation that might project the meaning that such a vocation is not a calling but rather a secular type of occupation. Furthermore, the term "non-professional missionary" is misleading when it is used for a "tentmaker," since tentmakers usually are members of a profession.[7]

Another expression which has been used for "tentmakers" is "the lay apostolate."[8] This term has merit in that it brings out the truth that Christian lay workers are to be witnesses who are sent by Christ, just as those who are ordained pastors. On the other hand, a difficulty arises with this term when one faces the fact that many *fully supported* missionaries are lay persons engaged in education, medicine, agriculture, relief work, and other services. They also could be referred to as "the lay apostolate." Therefore, this expression cannot be applied exclusively to "tentmakers."

Another term which has been recommended for this concept is "lay pastor."[9] This expression is close to that of a "lay reader" which many are acquainted with as someone who assists in worship services, but who is not ordained as a regular minister. On the other hand, this term has its limitations in that many tentmakers do not engage in services as pastors.

Another expression which has been used to describe such a person is a "self-supporting witness."[10] Even though this is a bit cumbersome, it does bring out the fact that a person in this category earns his or her own salary and yet at the same time is a witness for Jesus Christ. The expression "self-supporting witness" could include sharing the gospel with people of a different ethnic group, but the meaning is broader and therefore covers any type of witness, even among one's own family. It, therefore, can refer to any Christian lay person at home or abroad. An expression which carries the true meaning of the concept would be a "self-supporting cross-cultural witness." But this is unwieldy.

Another term which has been used is that of a "self-supporting missionary." This carries the significance of the concept very well, and people who hear this expression for the first time seem to grasp its meaning. One problem with the term "missionary" is the fact that it carries a certain stigma in various areas of the world as well as among people with syncretistic and universalistic views. Dr. Donald McGavran, who has been called the apostle of church growth, believes that in spite of the stigma involved, the term "missionary" should be reinstated to the position of honor it once held. Other terms used to express this concept include "lay missionaries."[11] But this can also refer to fully supported unordained missionaries. Professor Herbert Kane has also suggested the expression "ambassadors for Christ without portfolio." This however requires explanation. Another proffered appellation is "unofficial missionaries." But in touchy political situations this could be interpreted as a clandestine operation.

The one term which seems best to characterize the concept is that of "tentmaker." The apostle Paul, who thus supported himself, was the greatest missionary who ever lived. In Acts 18:1–5 we read, "Paul . . . came to Corinth and found a certain Jew named Aquila . . . lately come from Italy, with his wife Priscilla . . . . And because he was of the same craft, he abode with them, and wrought: for by their occupation they were tentmakers. And he . . . persuaded the Jews and the Greeks . . . that Jesus was Christ." But even though this expression, "tentmaker," is biblical, there are many Christians who do not understand its meaning, either because they do not know their Bibles well enough or they take the term literally to mean someone who is engaged in manufacturing tents. Perhaps with proper usage and popularization of this concept, more will come to grasp and appreciate its meaning.

Professor Herbert Kane defines such a "tentmaker" as "any dedicated Christian who lives and works overseas . . . and who uses his secular calling as an opportunity to give his personal witness to Jesus Christ."[12] Andrew Dymond gives this definition:

"The tentmaker is a missionary in terms of commitment, but is fully self-supporting."[13] Dr. Van Baak, who has been a missionary in Japan for many years with the Reformed Church, writes: "A Christian going overseas for any reason is potentially an ambassador for Jesus Christ." Dr. Ted Ward defines a tentmaker as one "witnessing for Christ while productively employed abroad."

There are more Protestant missionaries from North America serving overseas than ever before. The 1981 twelfth edition of the *Mission Handbook: North American Protestant Ministries Overseas* lists a total of 53,499. In spite of this, the computerized Christian organization, Intercristo, estimates that for every one of these missionaries there are over 100 other North Americans living and working overseas.

Statistics also bear this out. Figures from the Department of Commerce indicate that the number of Americans going overseas increased over ten times between 1960 and 1976.[14] The number of U.S. passports issued are a similar indicator. The U.S. Department of Commerce indicates that in 1950 300,000 such documents were provided by the government for American citizens,[15] but this rose in 1976 to 2,816,683 for one year.[16] This means that the number of U.S. passports issued during this period of sixteen years increased over nine times.[17] Another interesting figure is the fact that with U.S. passports being valid for five years, the total number in force between 1972–1976 was 13,022,683.[18] Since passports are not needed for U.S. citizens traveling overland to Canada and Mexico, the above figures reflect those who have gone overseas. For this reason, the American State Department holds that approximately two percent of the population (which is equal to over four million) reside abroad.

According to the Gallup poll, over one-third of the people in the United States claim to be born-again Christians. Even if one-fourth of those overseas were regenerated persons, this would bring the figure to around one million. Dr. W. Eugene Grubbs, the Foreign Mission Board consultant on laymen overseas, states, "The number of Southern Baptists among the Americans abroad . . . may be as high as 100,000 . . . . These . . . who take up residence abroad for varying periods of time constitute the greatest potential lay force in missions . . . if twentieth-century Christians will . . . work and give unashamed, unapologetic witness to the gospel."[19]

Many evangelical Christians from Canada, the British Isles,

Europe, Latin America, and other nations are also serving abroad in countries around the world. There are over 80,000 South Koreans working in Saudi Arabia, and the Christians among these have already started churches there. Even as God used the diaspora of the Jews throughout the world to be a witness to himself, so today there is a dispersion of Christians in practically every nation, believers who can be witnesses for the gospel of Jesus Christ.

This is an interesting fulfillment of the scriptural prophecy, " 'The people of God shall shine as brightly as the sun's brilliance, and those who turn many to righteousness will glitter like stars forever. But Daniel, keep this prophecy a secret; seal it up so that it will not be understood until the end times, when travel and education shall be vastly increased!' " (Dan. 12:3, 4, TLB). In a new sense we can also appreciate our Lord's statement to his disciples that they were "the light of the world" and "the salt of the earth." Or, as Bishop Stephen Neill says, "In the twentieth century one phenomenon has come into view which is incontestably new—for the first time there is in the world a universal religion, and that the Christian religion . . . . Christianity alone has acclimatized itself in every continent."[20] In fact, since there are Christians who are self-supporting scientists working even in Antarctica, tentmakers today can be lights in all seven continents.

Not only is there a dispersion of Christians all over the world, but the speed of intercommunication has rapidly increased. When my parents went as missionaries to Iran in 1919, the one-way trip took three months. Today it is possible to get there by SST in a matter of hours. Thus, the fact that we are living in a global village has fantastic implications for worldwide witness.

But what remains to be done? Two out of every three people in the world today still have not heard the gospel of Jesus Christ in a way that they can understand. If these who number just under three billion people are to be reached, both fully-supported and self-supported Christians need to be mobilized to carry out Christ's command. Dr. James Kennedy says, "Laymen are the most strategic and also the most unused key for the evangelization of the world."[21] Or as the Lausanne Covenant states in relation to the completion of Christ's commission, this "requires the whole church to take the whole gospel to the whole world."[22]

3/THE IMPRIMATUR OF SCRIPTURE

By their occupation they were tentmakers (Acts 18:3).

Next to the Apostle Paul, William Carey was probably the greatest self-supporting missionary who ever lived. It was he who clearly brought out that the Great Commission applied to every Christian. In his book which he published in 1792, *An Enquiry Into the Obligations of Christians to Use Means for the Conversion of the Heathen,*[1] he answers the argument that the command of Christ to teach all nations was restricted to the apostles. At Carey's time many held this view and therefore felt the Great Commission did not apply to them. In his book he points out that the command in Matthew 28:19 to evangelize the world is written along with the order to baptize. He therefore states that if our Lord's order to make disciples from among all nations only applied to those who actually heard him, then Christians in subsequent ages did not have the right to baptize either. But he conclusively shows that this cannot be the case because "If the command of Christ to teach all nations extends only to the apostles, then doubtless the promise of the divine presence in this work must be so limited; but this is worded in such a manner as expressly precludes such an idea. 'Lo, I am with you always, to the end of the world.' "[2] Thus our Lord gave the Great Commission to every Christian, whether he or she is a fully-supported or a self-supporting missionary.

Dr. Adoniram Judson Gordon, who was the founder of the college and seminary which today bear his name, used to explain the aim of Christ's Commission. He pointed out that it was not a matter of bringing the whole world to Christ, but rather of bringing Christ to the whole world. Our Lord himself said, "You are to go into all the world and preach the Good News to everyone, everywhere. Those who believe and are baptized will be saved. But those who refuse to believe will be condemned" (Mark 16:15, 16, TLB). In other words, not all will believe. William Carey further says that it is our obligation to disperse ourselves "into every country of the habitable globe and preach to all the inhabitants without exception or limitation." Speaking of Isaiah 60, Carey states that this passage indicates that business would be used for world evangelization. "The whole chapter is undoubtedly a prophecy that in the time of the glorious increase of the Church in the latter days, commerce shall subserve the spread of the gospel." Parts of the Scripture portion to which he refers state: "My people! Let your light shine for all nations to see! For the glory of the Lord is streaming from you . . . . All nations will come to your light . . . . Who are these that fly as a cloud and as doves to their windows? . . . Surely the isles shall wait for me and the ships of Tarshish . . . to bring thy sons from far, their silver and their gold with them, unto the name of the Lord thy God."[3]

Many of the godly men and women in the Old Testament were self-supporting witnesses. Even before the fall of man, God assigned work to Adam. "The Lord God placed the man in the Garden of Eden as its gardener, to tend and care for it" (Genesis 2:15, TLB). Thus, Adam was a cultivator, Abel was a sheep farmer, Abraham was a cattle raiser, Hagar was a domestic worker, Isaac was a farmer, Rebekah was a water carrier, Jacob was a roving rancher, Rachel was a sheep herder, Joseph was a premier, Miriam was a baby-sitter, Moses was a flock-grazer, Bezaleel was a skilled artificer, Joshua was a military commander, Rahab was an innkeeper, Deborah was a national deliverer, Gideon was a military leader, Samson was a champion fighter, Ruth was a gleaner, Boaz was a grain grower, David was a ruler, Asaph was a composer, Solomon was an emperor, the Queen of Sheba was an administrator, Job was a gentleman farmer, Amos was a sharecropper, Baruch was a writer, Daniel was a prime minister, Shadrach, Meshach, and Abednego were provincial administrators, Queen Esther was a ruler, and Nehemiah was a governor. Furthermore, many other God-fearing kings,

government officials, and military leaders are mentioned in the
Old Testament.

Also, in the New Testament our Lord's stepfather, Joseph, was
a carpenter, Martha was a housekeeper, Zacchaeus was a tax
collector, Nicodemus and Joseph of Arimathea were
supreme-court councillors, Barnabas was a landowner, Cornelius
was an officer, Luke was a doctor, Priscilla, Aquila, and Paul were
tentmakers, Lydia was a purple-dye seller, Zenas was a lawyer,
and Erastus was a city treasurer.

Even our Lord, though he was Creator of the universe, humbled
himself to become a self-supporting carpenter. As Sir Kenneth
Grubb has said of "tentmaking" service, "This is not a new thing.
It is as old as the carpenter's bench at Nazareth." But our Lord
also set his seal of approval on full-time missionary work, since
during his ministry he was supported by his friends. "Certain
women . . . and many others . . . ministered unto him of their
substance" (Luke 8:2, 3).

With the martyrdom of Stephen, persecution forced believers to
be scattered abroad. Those who "went everywhere preaching the
Word" were lay witnesses. The apostles stayed in Jerusalem.

The greatest prototype of a self-supporting witness was the
tentmaker Paul. When he and Barnabas were sent out from the
church in Antioch as missionaries, they paid their own way. And
it was while Paul was making tents with Aquila and Priscilla that
he led them to Christ. He described his self-supporting witness to
the Ephesian elders with these words: "I have not coveted
anyone's silver or gold or clothing. You yourselves know that
these hands of mine have supplied my own needs and the needs of
my companions. In everything I did, I showed you that by this
kind of hard work we must help the weak, remembering the
words the Lord Jesus himself said: It is more blessed to give than
to receive" (Acts 20:33-35, NIV).

Paul's primary purpose, however, was the spreading of the
good news about Jesus Christ, and his tentmaking was simply a
supporting role. As he stated, "I have preached the full Gospel of
Christ all the way from Jerusalem clear over into Illyricum. But
all the while my ambition has been to go still farther, preaching
where the name of Christ has never yet been heard, rather than
where a church has already been started by someone else. I have
been following the plan spoken of in the Scriptures where Isaiah
says that those who have never heard the name of Christ before

will see and understand" (Rom. 15:19–21, TLB).

The Apostle Paul also said, "Usually a person should keep on with the work he was doing when God called him" (1 Cor. 7:20, TLB). John Nevius and Roland Allen, who were missionaries in China, felt that this was an important principle to be observed in order for a church to become healthy and self-supporting. The danger was that those who came to Christ on the mission field would leave their former jobs and look to the missionaries to give them work and support. This, in many parts of the world, has resulted in an overdependence syndrome of the national Christians upon the mission and consequently has stunted the growth of many churches.

In 1 Corinthians 9, the Apostle Paul gives his apologia for self-supporting service. He had been accused of not being a bona fide apostle or missionary because he was a tentmaker. He states that the Corinthian Christians themselves were the proof or seal of his apostleship. He then goes on to point out that he rightly could have received support from the churches. He mentions that other apostles had been cared for by the Christians. He then asks facetiously, "Is it only I and Barnabas who must work for a living?" (1 Cor. 9:6, NIV).

Paul goes on to illustrate the validity of Christian workers receiving full support. He puts these questions to them: "Who serves as a soldier at his own expense? Who plants a vineyard and does not eat of its grapes? Who tends a flock and does not drink of the milk?" (1 Cor. 9:7, NIV). In other words, soldiers, farmers, and shepherds receive material benefits from their work. Also, in support of this, he cites the law of Moses: "Do not muzzle an ox when it is treading out the grain" (1 Cor. 9:9, NIV). While oxen were helping with the threshing, they were not to have their mouths muzzled, but were to be free to eat some of the harvest. Paul then explained that this law was given by God because of his concern for people. Laborers who work in the fields should have the right of sharing in the harvest. He then states, "If we have sown spiritual seed among you, is it too much if we reap a material harvest from you? If others have this right of support from you, shouldn't we have it all the more?" (1 Cor. 9:11, 12, NIV). Paul adds that even though they would have been justified in receiving support, they purposely chose to go without it in order not to hinder the spread of the gospel of Christ and so to make its acceptance absolutely free.

The apostle also points out that Jewish priests working in the temple received their food and support from the offerings. He then draws this conclusion from these references: "In the same way, the Lord has commanded that those who preach the gospel should receive their living from the gospel" (1 Cor. 9:14, NIV). As Bishop Stephen Neil says of this passage, "It was laid down as a clear principle that those who serve the gospel with all their time and strength had a right to be maintained from the gospel, and that therefore responsibility for their support rested on the church."⁴ Thus we see the Apostle Paul clearly believed in and taught the validity of fully-supported missionaries.

But he had voluntarily decided to forego the right to financial support from other Christians. He mentions that he was not writing this as a hint to gain their support. He states that his pay or reward was the satisfaction of preaching the gospel without expense to anyone. He voluntarily had made himself a slave to serve others in order to win as many as possible for Christ. For this same reason he had purposely identified himself with various groups in order to win them to Christ, as he adds, "I have become all things to all men so that by all possible means I might save some" (1 Cor. 9:22, NIV). Scripturally, self-supporting service should go right along with full-time missionary ministries. Reflecting this biblical principal further, Phillip Butler, founder of Intercristo, observes, "It is just as valid for missionaries to support themselves as it is to have churches supporting them financially."

It is interesting to note that the Apostle Paul also at times accepted support from Christians. In his second letter to the Corinthians he wrote,

Was it a sin for me to lower myself in order to elevate you by preaching the gospel of God to you free of charge? I robbed other churches by receiving support from them so as to serve you. And when I was with you and needed something, I was not a burden to anyone, for the brothers who came from Macedonia supplied what I needed. I have kept myself from being a burden to you in any way and will continue to do so (2 Cor. 11:7-9, NIV).

The Christian financial support Paul received while he was at Corinth was probably from the church in Philippi. He referred to these gifts in his letter to them.

*How grateful I am and how I praise the Lord that you are helping
me again. I know that you have always been anxious to send what
you could . . . you have done right in helping me in my present
difficulty. As you well know, when I first brought the Gospel to you
and then went on my way, leaving Macedonia, only you Philippians
became my partners in giving and receiving. No other church did
this. Even when I was over in Thessalonica you sent help twice. But
though I appreciate your gifts, what makes me happiest is the
well-earned reward you will have because of your kindness. At the
moment I have all I need—more than I need! I am generously
supplied with the gifts you sent me* (Phil. 4:10, 14–18, TLB).

In this passage we see that Paul was not so rigid in his policy of
paying his own way by tentmaking work that he would not
receive support from Christians who sincerely wanted to back his
ministry.

But on the other hand, if he felt that securing financial help
from others would restrict the effectiveness of his ministry or
would be misinterpreted, he did not take it. This is the reason he
wrote to the Christians in Corinth, "I will not be a burden to you
because what I want is not your possessions but you. After all,
children should not have to save up for their parents, but parents
for their children. So I will very gladly spend for you everything I
have and expend myself as well" (2 Cor. 12:14–16, NIV).

In his letter to the Ephesian church, the Apostle Paul further
brings out the important part that lay Christians play. He
mentions that when our Lord ascended on high to his position of
power, he gave gifts to his Church in the form of Christian
leaders: apostles, prophets, evangelists, pastors, and teachers. The
purpose of their ministry was "for the equipping of the saints for
the work of service, to the building up of the body of Christ"
(Eph. 4:12, NASB). Thus, the scriptural principle for
fully-supported officers is for them to assist self-supporting
Christians in carrying on the work of Christ's Church. The two
must together work cooperatively. In this same letter Paul tells
how self-supporting witnesses can contribute to those who are in
need. "He who has been stealing must steal no longer, but must
work, doing something useful with his hands, that he may have
something to share with those in need" (Eph. 4:28, NIV).

Paul further testifies to the spiritual effectiveness of Christians,
who were self-supporting witnesses since they had only recently

come to Christ, when he writes to the church in Thessalonica, "From you sounded out the word of the Lord not only in Macedonia and Achaia, but also in every place your faith to God-ward is spread abroad, so that we need not to speak anything" (1 Thes. 1:8). Here too he mentions to them the tentmaking ministry he carried on in their midst. "Surely you remember, brothers, our toil and hardship; we worked night and day in order not to be a burden to anyone while we preached the gospel of God to you" (1 Thes. 2:9, NIV). He then reiterates the same fact in his second letter to them. "We were not idle when we were with you, nor did we eat anyone's food without paying for it. On the contrary, we worked night and day laboring and toiling so that we would not be a burden to any of you. We did this, not because we do not have the right to such help, but in order to make ourselves a model for you to follow" (2 Thes. 3:7–9, NIV). This shows that as a working self-supporting witness, Paul was an example for other believers to do the same. He was able to go on and speak with authority: "For even when we were with you, we gave you this rule: 'If a man will not work, he shall not eat.' We hear that some of you are idle. They are not busy; they are busybodies. Such people we command and urge in the Lord Jesus Christ, to settle down and earn the bread they eat" (2 Thes. 3:10–12, NIV). The Apostle Paul was a prototype of what the true Christian tentmaker should be.

As Sir Kenneth Grubb has said of self-supporting witness for Christ, "This method bears the imprimatur of Scripture."

4/THE HISTORY OF TENTMAKING

Others have labored, and you have entered into their labor (John 4:38, NASB).

In the early church it was the lay Christians who, because of the persecution in Jerusalem, "went everywhere preaching the Word." From then on throughout the pages of church history, God has not only used fully-supported Christians to extend his gospel, but also tentmakers.

TENTMAKERS FROM THE CHURCH OF THE EAST

Under the persecution of Christians by Zoroastrians in Persia between A.D. 339 and 448, hundreds of thousands were martyred. Many were also exiled. These, like those in the early church, went everywhere preaching the gospel. Most of them were lay people who had to work for their living.[1] "Supporting themselves by the labor of their own hands or filling appointments as secretaries, physicians, or stewards in the households of the nobles and princes of those lands to which they went, they were one and all missionaries of the cross."[2] The secret of their power was their knowledge of the Word of God. "They were men of great faith, mighty in Scriptures, large portions of which they knew by heart."[3] Many even memorized the whole New Testament. They supported themselves and yet their main vocation was that of being ambassadors for Christ.

According to Dr. John Stewart, who spent many years studying this movement, these Christians constituted "the most missionary church the world has ever seen."[4] He supports this view with the evidence that through their vast evangelistic activity there were more people in the eleventh century in Asia who called themselves Christians than there were in all of Europe. He mentions that with their evangelistic zeal they spread the gospel throughout Central Asia, India, China, Korea, Japan, and even Southeast Asia. "Afghanistan and Tibet, which are spoken of today as lands still closed to the Gospel message, were centers of Christian activity long before even Mohammed was born."[5] Wherever they went, they established schools for the training of children in the Christian communities. Even their monasteries were in reality missionary Bible institutes, since the main subject taught was the Scriptures of the Old and New Testaments.[6]

The question naturally arises, Why don't we hear more about this great missionary movement in Asia? One reason is the fact that differences in doctrine between the Eastern and Western churches resulted in Europeans writing off the Nestorians and other Christians in Asia as heretics. Bishop Stephen Neill states, "Almost all church history has been presented exclusively from the Western point of view. After Chalcedon in 451, the Eastern churches simply ceased to exist."[7] Many Christian scholars now realize that the Nestorian doctrine was not as heretical as was supposed, and that religious politics played an important part in this disassociation and the consequent historical omission.

Another question that arises is, Why was Christianity almost completely wiped out in Asia? One explanation is the fact that Scriptures usually were kept in the ancient languages and therefore were not understood by the common people. The churches then became ceremonial and nominal in their faith. Thus Islam and Buddhism were able over the centuries to assimilate those people who had been Christians and finally to eradicate their faith.

TENTMAKERS IN ROMAN CATHOLIC MISSIONS

When Marco Polo (1254–1323) went to China in the latter part of the thirteenth century, the extension of Christianity was one of the motives for his travels. Recent scholarship has also shown that Christopher Columbus likewise was impelled in his explorations by a desire to discover a better way to India for the purpose of

Christianizing the people there. "Christopher Columbus was one of the most remarkable Christian laymen of all time," writes August J. Kling. "His voyage to America was the realization of a vision drawn entirely from the Holy Scriptures. *The Book of Prophecies,* written by Columbus, was a careful compilation of all the teachings of the Bible on the subject of the earth, distant lands, seas, population movements, undiscovered tribes, prophecies of the future spread of the gospel throughout the whole world, prophecies of travel between distant places, prophecies of the end of the world and the establishment of the earthly kingdom of Jesus Christ as King of Kings and Lord of Lords. He believed that Christ's return and the formation of His universal kingdom could not take place until all nations and tribes of the distant isles had been evangelized."[8]

Francis Xavier (1506–1552), one of the greatest missionaries who ever lived, called on the students of France to give up their small ambitions and to come East to preach the gospel. He was so concerned for the conversion of peoples of the world that he got the King of Portugal to require his lay Portuguese governors in India to do all they could to bring the local population under their authority into the Catholic Church. Jesuit missionaries in Japan supported themselves by the silk trade as a means of carrying on their missionary activities. Also Roman Catholic missions in Spanish America engaged in agriculture and ranching for their livelihood.[9]

CHAPLAINS OF THE EAST INDIA COMPANY

When the East India Company began, Sir Thomas Rowe was its first ambassador to the Mogul Court from 1607–1612. Since he was a dedicated Christian, he was accompanied by his chaplain. The East India Company then continued to secure clergy to minister to its employees. Working regulations were issued instructing these chaplains to learn the local languages in order to make the Christian faith known to the national people. But usually the Company disregarded this provision and in practice often opposed missionary work.[10]

A number of dedicated ministers who were influenced by the Evangelical Awakening went out under the East India Company. The best known of these "pious chaplains" was the Rev. Henry

Martyn (1781–1812). Before going to India he had the opportunity of meeting the great Christian social reformer, William Wilberforce (1759–1833). He also was able to get advice from John Newton (1725–1807), the former slave trader who after his conversion became a Christian pastor and wrote the hymn "Amazing Grace." Henry Martyn had first considered going to India as a missionary, but decided to go as a chaplain mainly for two reasons. First, he did not have the support necessary, and this would give him a regular salary. Secondly, the East India Company at that time was not allowing missionary work within its domains.

On the sailing ship going out, he was so shocked by the behavior of the other British passengers and crew that he wrote, "May these poor wretched countrymen who sail with me, whom I see under the power of Satan, be turned away from their sin to God."[11] When he landed at Calcutta in 1806, he reportedly said, "I have lived more like a clod of dirt than like a son of God. Now let me burn out for Christ." He literally did this, since he lived only six more years.

Along with having an effective ministry with the British subjects in the employ of the East India Company, he was able to learn the language of the area and minister to the local people as well. He translated the New Testament into Hindustani. Furthermore, he produced a revision of the Arabic New Testament. In 1811 he went to Shiraz in southern Iran. While there he completed a translation of the Persian New Testament in eight months. He then had local calligraphers write out a copy by hand which was then presented to the Shah. Heading for his home leave in England, he then traveled on through Turkey, but was so worn out by disease and exhaustion that he died in Tokat October 6, 1812, at thirty-one years of age. Rarely has the world seen such a combination of dedicated devotion and superior scholarship.

THE MORAVIAN TENTMAKERS

Throughout history, revivals have usually resulted in missionary awakenings. This was true of the Moravians. In 1727 God poured forth his Spirit in answer to prayer on these religious refugees who were gathered at Herrnhut, in what is now East Germany, under

Count Zinzendorf (1700–1760). While he was attending the coronation of the Danish King Christian VI, his cousin by marriage, he met a black slave from the West Indies who told him of the spiritual and physical misery of his people on the island of St. Thomas. He shared this need with the Moravians, and two artisans immediately volunteered to go there as self-supporting missionaries. They were Leonhard Dober, a potter, and David Nitschmaun, a carpenter. They arrived in the West Indies in 1732 and supported themselves by their trades.[12] Thus began the significant spiritual movement under which the Moravians "were called to shoulder their artisan's tools and follow the Lamb in a mission to the world."[13]

Another group of Moravian missionaries went to Labrador. They were supported entirely by income earned by trading with the Eskimos. They even owned their own ships with which to carry on their commerce. They made modest profit margins, which were completely devoted to the work of the mission, and made it possible for them to administer welfare to Eskimos who were poor, sick, and old. Furthermore, during hard winters and poor hunting and fishing seasons, they were able to provide assistance from their trade stores for those who were suffering from economic hardship. This principle of self-support also enabled them to teach the people whom they were serving the dignity of labor.

Two of their missionaries went to Surinam (Dutch Guiana) in Latin America and started working there as tailors in 1754. As others joined them, a business, bakery, and watchmaking industry were added. These enterprises enabled them to hire local employees who were not only given jobs but also were led to a saving knowledge of Jesus Christ. The name of the firm was Christoph Kersten & Co. This title meant "Christ-bearer Christian and Company." The latter word stood for the Unity of the Brethren or the Moravians. Today this organization is the largest trading company in Surinam, with branches in New York, Amsterdam, and Hamburg. The yearly contributions of this company to the church amount to hundreds of thousands of dollars.[14]

The Moravians argued that voluntary contributions were inadequate for the size of the missionary task. Therefore, missionaries needed to be supported and augmented through business enterprises which also would be opportunities for

Christian witness. Believers practicing their faith in the
marketplace could be living audio-visual aids to missions.[15] For
example, the C. Kersten & Co. in Surinam provided old-age
pensions and medical insurance for their workers long before this
was done in North America. Furthermore, they held in-service
training courses for their employees as well as assisting them with
the purchase of their own homes. Nor was the spiritual dimension
forgotten. Each working day began with a time of devotions. By
1926 there were 13,000 members in the Moravian congregation in
Surinam.[16] And this company has continued now for over 200
years.

Dr. William Danker concludes, "The most important
contribution of the Moravians was their emphasis that every
Christian is a missionary and should witness through his daily
vocation. If the example of the Moravians had been studied more
carefully by other Christians, it is possible that the businessman
might have retained his honored place within the expanding
Christian world mission, beside the preacher, teacher, and
physician."[17]

THE COBBLER WHO BECAME THE FATHER OF THE MODERN MISSIONARY MOVEMENT

"My business is to witness for Christ," said William Carey
(1761–1834). "I make shoes just to pay my expenses."[18] This
statement summed up his life principles as he continued to
support himself and those working with him on the mission field
as a tentmaker in India. Before he left England, he had told the
Christians who had agreed to support him that his leaving them
was like one going with ropes down into a mine. He pleaded with
them to continue holding the ropes. However, when he got to
Calcutta, the people back home forgot him financially. He
furthermore was faced by official opposition from the East India
Company, which threatened to deport him. He therefore took his
family into the interior of the country and worked as manager of
an indigo plantation. By associating with the local people in this
position, he learned the Bengali language. Within five years he had
completed the translation of the New Testament into Bengali, even
though later on he revised this seven more times to get as good a
version as possible.

In 1799, six years after Carey had first arrived in India, he was joined by Joshua Marshman, a schoolteacher, and William Ward, a printer. This triumvirate became one of the most famous missionary teams in history. Because of British hostility, they had to settle sixteen miles up the river from Calcutta in the Danish colony of Serampore. These three self-supporting missionaries translated and published the whole Bible into six different languages, the New Testament into twenty-three others and portions of the Scriptures in ten more tongues.[19]

William Carey also became a leading Sanskrit scholar. He was invited to become professor of this language at Fort William College in Calcutta. For this position he was given a large salary, but 95% of it went into the support of the mission. He also published a fine Sanskrit grammar of 1,000 pages. Furthermore, he became a leading authority on the botany of India and wrote articles on this for the *Encyclopedia Brittanica.*

He was also instrumental in getting laws passed forbidding the sacrificing of girl babies in the Ganges River. And he brought about legislation outlawing the killing of widows on their husband's funeral pyres. In addition, he established Christian schools and churches.

In his historic book, *An Enquiry Into the Obligations of Christians to Use Means for the Conversion of the Heathens,* he planned for the evangelization of the whole world. This publication, which he wrote before going to India and put out in 1792, lists facts and figures for the nations of the world as he knew them. He even planned a missionary congress for worldwide evangelization. But because he was so far ahead of his time others did not go along with his vision, and therefore this did not materialize. In 1833 he wrote about tentmaking: "We have ever held it to be an essential principle in the conduct of missions, that whenever it is practicable, missionaries should support themselves in whole or in part through their own exertions."[20]

He was also careful to give credit to God for what was accomplished. Just before his death, different ones were talking about all he had done. He humbly requested of them, "Don't talk about William Carey. But talk about William Carey's Lord." Even though he never returned to England, he was knighted by the British government. Also the present Indian government, though a secular state, paid tribute to this great man of God with a commemorative stamp issued in 1961 on the bicentennial of his birth.

OTHER NINETEENTH-CENTURY TENTMAKERS

Robert Morrison (1782–1834) tried in the early 1800s to go as a witness to China. However, the East India Company refused him permission to go on any of their shipping. For this reason he had to come to the United States, cross the continent by land, and then take a sailing ship from the West Coast to China. He was able to work on the island of Macao, not far from Hong Kong. He studied the language diligently and finally became an interpreter for the East India Company, which had originally denied him passage. Morrison thereby earned his own support. He also secretly translated the whole Bible into Chinese. His grave can be seen today on the island of Macao, where he died.

A German Christian named Johannes Emde went to Indonesia as a watchmaker in 1811. Having married a Javanese wife, he was able to preach the gospel to her relatives and to other contacts. He planted a Christian church there and in 1843 brought thirty-five Muslim converts to a minister for baptism.[21]

Another tentmaker by the name of Captain William LeLacheur, who was an English sea merchant, established the first Protestant church in Costa Rica in 1848. He also greatly assisted the economic growth of that country. Besides establishing the coffee trade between Costa Rica and the British Isles, he supplied scholarships for young Costa Ricans to be educated in England. These then returned to become leaders in the development of their country. Captain LeLacheur furthermore distributed Scriptures throughout Costa Rica for the British and Foreign Bible Society.

MILITARY TENTMAKERS

The Rev. Justin Perkins, who was the first American missionary to northwestern Iran, wrote, "Among the English who are scattered throughout the East there is a large number of devotedly pious men, military and civil officers of high standing, who are not ashamed to be known as the humble servants of God as well as the faithful servants of their country. Such are missionary pioneers, rapidly preparing the way for the spread of the gospel."[22]

Some of the earliest witnesses in Afghanistan were Christian officers and soldiers in the British army during the First and Second Anglo-Afghan Wars. Captain Reban of the occupation force in Kabul, along with other like-minded men of God, in 1838 ordered a shipment of Pashtu Bibles, which William Carey had translated and printed. They wanted to distribute these among the Afghans. When a caravan of Scriptures arrived from Calcutta, it created much official consternation. "It would disturb the tribesmen and stir up fanaticism," declared the authorities. "The Bibles must be returned at once." The orders were obeyed, but the Scriptures never got back. The returning caravan was attacked in the passes and looted, and thus the Word of God was distributed in Afghanistan.[23] Also, among the British Christian servicemen stationed at Herat in Western Afghanistan there was an earnest prayer fellowship. One officer, a physician by the name of Dr. Logan, was able to distribute William Carey's New Testament in Pashtu and Henry Martyn's in Persian to different Afghan friends.

Another group of British Christian officers in Peshawar on the Northwest Frontier of India prayed for the opening of that area to missionaries and sought permission for this. Herbert Edwardes, the Christian Commissioner of this province answered, "I see no difficulty in the matter of founding a Mission. We protect the Hindu and Mohammedan in the enjoyment of their religion. It is the primary duty of a Christian to preach the gospel of Christ."[24] Consequently a public meeting was held to establish the work on December 19, 1853. Edwardes, who was later knighted and promoted to general, chaired the meeting. In his address he said:

It is not for the Government to proselytize India. The duty of evangelizing India lies at the door of private Christians. Every English man and every English woman in India is answerable to do what he can towards fulfilling it. This day we are met to do so —to provide the best means we can for spreading the gospel. In this crowded city we may hear the Brahaman in his temple sound his "sunkh" and gong; the Muezzin on his lofty minaret fill the air with the "auzan"; and the civil government which protects them both will take upon itself the duty of protecting the Christian missionary who goes forth to preach the gospel.[25]

In speaking of General Sir Herbert Edwardes, the report of the newly founded mission stated:

A more successful administration of a more difficult frontier tract of country in more perilous times has been rarely witnessed. His government has been . . . characterized by the highest moral character, by decision, gentleness and power which has given him amongst the people themselves the appellation of a model ruler.[26]

A school was started by the mission in Peshawar and was given the name of this military man of God. Still today it exists as Edwardes College.

TENTMAKERS FROM THE SWISS BASEL MISSION

The Basel Mission encouraged its workers to be self-supporting. For example, John Haller, a master weaver, was sent out to India in 1851. In less than two years, he had over twenty looms in operation and was employing twenty-seven workers. Trying to develop dyes that would not fade, he discovered that he could make khaki color from the sap of the semecarpus tree. He gave it this name because in the local language "khaki" means the color of dust. Lord Roberts of Kandahar visited the weaving establishment and was impressed with this dye. As commander-in-chief of the forces in India, he had the British Army replace redcoats with khaki-colored uniforms. With the prospering of the weaving work in India, employees were able to build comfortable cottages and have their own gardens. They also participated in a workers' credit union and a health insurance plan. As a Christian industry, daily devotions were held in the factory.[27]

The Basel Mission also established a trading company in the West African area of Ghana. Three Swiss farmers who were members of the Mission were the first to introduce the cocoa plant into that country. It had originally come from South America. The first shipment of cocoa from Ghana was sent to Europe in 1891 by the Basel Mission. Twenty years after this, Ghana had become the leading cocoa-producing country in the world, and the per capita income had become the highest of any nation in black Africa.

The Basel Mission sought to do everything possible to show that "godliness is profitable unto all things, having promise of the life that now is, and of that which is to come" (1 Tim. 4:8). In areas where they were not able to open a mission station, the company would start a trading post where its business staff would also witness. The Mission worked on the premise that the office of a preacher was not the only type of spiritual service. They believed that the person who is filled with the Spirit of God is spiritual, no matter what branch of God's work he or she is in.

Dr. Danker writes, "The Basel Trading Company has always sought to send out high-quality Christians to make their witness in the marketplace. They have not hid their light under a bushel . . . . They set it high upon the candlestick of a living demonstration of the Gospel in the factory and across the counter."[28]

TENTMAKERS FOR CHRIST IN JAPAN

Captain Janes, who was a graduate of West Point, was invited in 1871 to head up a military school at Kumamoto in western Japan. Within five years his Christian influence had been so great that thirty-five of his students not only accepted Christ but took an oath of loyalty to the Lord. As Christians they sought the emancipation of their nation. Most of them were from the Samurai class and came to be known as the Kumamoto Band. They had a great impact upon Japan. One of their number, Dr. Paul Kanamori, became a great evangelist.

Another Christian tentmaker who went to Japan was Dr. Clark. In 1876 he was invited by the Japanese government to start an agricultural school on the northern island of Hokkaido. Before the end of the year, the whole first class of fifteen students in the agricultural school accepted Christ and sought baptism. The second year, he and the other students led the next class to Christ as well.[29]

TENTMAKERS BACK
THE STUDENT VOLUNTEER MOVEMENT

One of the greatest missionary thrusts in history began with the Student Volunteer Movement, which was initiated at a conference convened by Dwight L. Moody at Mount Hermon, Massachusetts, during the summer of 1886. They had as their slogan, "The evangelization of the world in this generation." This movement also had outstanding lay leadership in Dr. Robert E. Speer and Dr. John R. Mott. Over twenty thousand men and women actually went to the mission fields of the world under this banner. Christian businessmen in 1906 met to pray for missions and were led to set up the Laymen's Missionary Movement. Within three years this organization had over thirty-five hundred offices in

North America with over one hundred thousand attending meetings in seventy-five cities across the continent. They also quadrupled the giving for missions. As Roberta Winter has written, "It was these businessmen and their wives in thousands of women's missionary societies . . . which provided the much needed money to send the youth who were on fire to go."[30]

A RUSSIAN CHRISTIAN TENTMAKER

Jenny de Mayer started working as a self-supporting Red Cross nurse in Russian Central Asia in 1910. She even tried to get into Afghanistan but was refused permission. However, she gave Scriptures to Afghans who had come across the border into Russia, and she rejoiced to see the Bibles and portions packed in their traveling bags to take back with them into Afghanistan. The plight of the Muslim pilgrims who were on their way to Mecca so touched her that she got permission to be a nurse on a ship which took "Hajjis" from the Black Sea through the Mediterranean and into the Red Sea to Jidda. As she ministered lovingly to the sick and to the dying, she constantly wore her nurse's uniform with the red cross. She even established a dispensary in Jidda, the port for Mecca. The fascinating account of her ministry is recorded in her book, *Adventures with God.*[31] She then traveled back to Tashkent via Mashad, Iran in 1922. Finally she was arrested by Communist authorities in Tashkent and put in Soviet prisons for over eight years. In spite of awful conditions, she had freedom to help and to witness to the other inmates. Once when she was being transferred from one prison to another, a Russian woman in jail with her said, "Comrade de Mayer, as you go from us, we feel as if Jesus Christ is leaving us." Because of the expressed concern of Christians around the world for her, the Soviet authorities finally released her and she was allowed to retire in Canada. Throughout her ministry she took the name "Shaheeda," which meant "witness." She truly was a joyful witness for Christ, and not only gladly suffered for her Lord but supported herself in his service throughout Russia, Central Asia, and Arabia.

5/TENTMAKING BY NON-CHRISTIANS

The citizens of this world are more clever . . . than the godly are (Luke 16:8).

The local Jewish Rabbi in Kabul, Afghanistan, along with carrying on his religious duties, also works as a businessman. This conforms to rabbinical tradition. In the same way, the Apostle Paul was a tentmaker along with his spiritual service. Through the centuries, rabbinical training has encouraged a supplemental profession which has enabled the Jewish people to have pastoral care available throughout the world, even in places where their numbers are too small to support a rabbi.

Employing the method of self-support, Muslims also have spread their religion principally through soldiers, traders, and government administrators. It is mainly because of this method that their adherents today number one-sixth of the population of the world. Even though Islam currently has fully-supported missionaries in various countries, the main thrust of its extension around the world is being carried on by its self-supporting laity. Dr. Van Halsema writes, "A resurgent Islam linked with political power in many Muslim countries also is determined to revive the missionary zeal which brought millions of people under the sway of their faith."[1] For example, a new tentmaking organization for Muslim propagation has been established. It is called *Tablighi Jamaat,* or the "preaching association," and has its headquarters in Rai Wind, near Lahore, Pakistan. Its goal is to strengthen Islam among its own people through calling them back to Allah and to faithfulness in prayer, fasting, witnessing, giving of alms, going on pilgrimage, and reading the Koran. It also aims at propagating the Muslim faith throughout the world. As a self-supporting lay movement, members insist on paying their own way and will not even accept a free cup of tea. They contribute one month of their time each year to attend conventions and to go out with teams on preaching tours.

Recently a student from Mecca, studying petroleum engineering at Harvard, was invited to a Christian home for a weekend. Early in the morning he knocked on the bedroom door of his hosts to ask the direction of Mecca so he could face it in prayer. He also talked about Islam with everyone he met. Muslims often put Christians to shame by their zeal.

Communism has also spread through lay propagandists. This movement, which has been called a heresy of Christianity, has adopted the scriptural principle of disseminating its doctrines through tentmakers. In Afghanistan, students from both Russia and China came to study at the University of Kabul. They did not come because of its academic standing. Really, they were missionaries from their respective countries. It was not long before most of the students at the Kabul University openly declared themselves to be Communists.

The Mormons are using the tentmaking principle to increase conversions to their religion. At present they have 26,500 young men who give two years of their lives to be missionaries.[2] Usually, they themselves or their families pay their way, and thus the cost to the headquarters in Salt Lake City is negligible. Special language classes are also given the young people who are going where a different tongue is spoken. These missionaries succeed in converting approximately one out of every 1,000 strangers they contact. For example, with 1,600 of their missionaries active in Great Britain, the membership of the Mormons there has increased from 9,500 thirteen years ago to 80,000 at present. Mormons, with their missionaries serving worldwide, increased their membership by 50 percent during the decade from 1965 to 1975.[3] It is little wonder that President Carter, in speaking to the Southern Baptist Convention which has just under 3,000 missionaries, referred to the Mormon missionary movement, and added, "Compared to our great potential, our achievements are small indeed."

All members of the Jehovah's Witnesses are considered

ministers. This is the reason for their extensive activity, door to door and on the streets. They now number approximately two million adherents in over 200 countries. Mainly through the zealous use of the tentmaking principle, their church around the world increased by 34 percent in 1974 alone.[4]

When Dr. Kenneth Strachan was director of the Latin America Mission, he realized that with the methods being used it would be hundreds of years before Christians could evangelize even a small country like Costa Rica. He therefore studied the means employed in the spread of Islam, Communism, Mormonism and the ideas of Jehovah's Witnesses. His research resulted in the thesis that any movement is successful in proportion to its mobilizing all of its membership in the continual propagation of its doctrines. From this principle he developed Evangelism-in-Depth. It has been variously called "In-Depth Evangelism," "New Life for All," "Here's Life," or "Saturation Evangelism." Dr. Strachan came to see the importance of mobilizing all of the self-supporting laity in the churches for successful evangelistic thrusts, and he learned this from non-Christian movements which had adopted the scriptural principle of tentmaking.

6/THE SPIRIT TOLD ME TO GO

The Holy Spirit told me to go . . . (Acts 11:12, TLB).

Along with other Christians, in the spring of 1947 I too applied
for a teaching position in Afghanistan. This appeared to be in line
with the Lord's leading in my life. Being born into a missionary
family in Tabriz, Iran, just eighty miles below the Russian border
at the Caucasus, as a boy I remember hearing the Christians in
the little church there praying for the closed country of
Afghanistan a thousand miles to the east. Although I cannot
pinpoint the day of my conversion, when I was twelve years old I
joined the church on confession of faith and know that I was born
again before that time.

Having come to the States for my high school and college, I
was a sophomore at Princeton University when America entered
World War II. Since so many men were in the service,
Inter-Varsity needed male staff workers and therefore in 1943,
while I was still in college preparing for the chaplaincy, I was
invited to work for them visiting universities throughout New
York State and New England on weekends. This continued
through my study in seminary.

Once when Inter-Varsity General Secretary Stacey Woods was
visiting Princeton, he had so many interviews that the only way to
talk with him was to buy a ticket on the train and ride to the next
station. I shared with him my increasing concern for missions.
With World War II nearly over, it seemed that Christians would
have an unprecedented opportunity to evangelize the whole world

and students could be a crucial factor in this. Much to my
amazement, I was invited to be Inter-Varsity's missionary
secretary for the United States and Canada. I went to Chicago
during the spring of 1945 to take on these new responsibilities.
Since I was still a student, I was entitled to live in the
International House at the University of Chicago. There my eyes
were opened to the tremendous evangelistic opportunity with
foreign students in this country. Bob Finley, who was also on the
staff of Inter-Varsity, moved into International House with me and
we saw students from other countries readily come to a saving
knowledge of Jesus Christ. Later, Bob Finley started International
Students Incorporated, which is engaged in this vital ministry
today.[1]

When the Student Volunteer Movement started under Dwight
L. Moody and Robert Wilder at Mt. Hermon, Massachusetts,
during the summer of 1886, its goal was "the evangelization of the
world in this generation." God raised up leaders such as Robert
E. Speer, John R. Mott, and Samuel M. Zwemer. Thousands,
including my parents, went to the mission fields of the world
under this movement. However, as new leadership took over after
World War I and as critical views of the Scripture were adopted,
the original missionary vision of the Student Volunteer Movement
was lost, and it finally voted itself out of existence. Therefore
another organization, the Student Foreign Missions Fellowship,
was started in 1936 to continue challenging young people with the
need for worldwide evangelization. In 1945 this joined with the
Inter-Varsity Christian Fellowship and became the missionary arm
of that organization. This merger was greatly assisted by Dr.
Robert McQuilkin, the founder and president of Columbia Bible
College, and by Wilbert Norton, who had been a charter member
of the Student Foreign Missions Fellowship and was now on
furlough from his service in Africa. After graduation from
seminary, I therefore was able to spend full time as missionary
secretary of the combined organization.

Since God had used the quadrennial missionary conventions of
the Student Volunteer Movement in such a powerful way in the
past, it was felt that a similar conference should be planned.
World War II having just ended, mission fields that had been
closed during the hostilities were now open. The time therefore
seemed right to challenge students with opportunities around the
world and to pray that the Lord would send forth the laborers of

his choosing. I visited campuses across Canada and the United States, presenting this need and inviting students to come to the Convention for Missionary Advance to be held at the University of Toronto just after Christmas and over New Year's Day 1946–47.

In speaking to students, I reminded them of the way our Lord prayed all night before he chose his disciples. I then asked the question why we did not have all-night prayer meetings for laborers. As I said this, the Holy Spirit convicted me of hypocrisy. I had never spent a night in prayer. Therefore when I was visiting Prairie Bible Institute in Three Hills, Alberta, during March of 1946, I determined to pray overnight asking God to call the laborers of his choosing and seeking to know more clearly what he wanted me to do. I planned to divide the night into half-hour periods, alternating between studying the Scriptures and praying. Shortly before this I had read a statement by Robert Wilder in which he wrote that the Bible study which had been the greatest blessing in his life was the time he traced the person and work of the Holy Spirit from Genesis to Revelation. I therefore decided to do the same. The study proved to be very rich indeed and gave me a fuller realization and appreciation of the third person of the Godhead and his work. Toward morning, as I was praying and asking the Lord what he would have me do, I did not hear an audible voice, but the question came into my mind from the Lord, "Are you willing to do anything for me?" When I agreed, another question came from him, "Are you willing even to die for me?" I prayed, "Lord, you died for me; therefore I will gladly die for thee." Completely and unexpectedly the power of God came upon me in waves as I was baptized in the Holy Spirit. His love, joy, peace, and other fruit was multiplied in my life. And when I spoke to the school in the morning assembly, God worked in a new way. More students than ever responded to the challenge.

From then on through the missionary convention it was not all smooth sailing. We were plagued by shortages of funds. And yet God supplied all our needs. The coming conference was also attacked by liberals who accused us of splitting away and establishing a work outside the mainstream of the Church. Also, separatist Christians threatened to boycott the Convention unless the invitation for Dr. Samuel Zwemer to speak were cancelled, since they had found a quotation from Karl Barth in one of his books. To solve this difficulty amicably, Dr. Zwemer graciously signed his agreement with Inter-Varsity's basis of faith and thus continued on the program. The threat was not put into effect.

Then, just before the Convention, one of the main speakers, Bakht Singh from India, slipped on the ice, receiving a compound fracture in the elbow of his right arm. He got permission from the doctors to wait on his operation until after he had given his message. This meant that he endured much pain, but he triumphantly said that this kept him awake every night so that he could pray more for God's will to be done in the lives of the students.

At the opening meeting, the official representative of the University of Toronto, who had been asked to welcome the Convention, took the opportunity to attack evangelicals. Dr. Harold Ockenga, who spoke right after him, was wonderfully able to answer his charges. Also, representatives of the Student Christian Movement, who were invited to attend as observers, wrote a highly critical attack on the Convention, stating that it was a combination of outdated theology and high-pressure emotionalism. God nevertheless worked mightily, and Inter-Varsity records show that over half of the 575 students who attended actually ended up going to mission fields around the world. These included Jim Elliot, David Howard, and Ralph Winter, who all later left for Latin America. Half a dozen from this Convention went as tentmakers to Afghanistan after that country early in 1947 issued the invitation for teachers to enter. In 1948, this student missionary convention moved to Urbana, Illinois, in order to be more centrally located in North America.

At this time I felt led of the Lord to send in an application to teach in Afghanistan. However, some of my best Christian friends sought to dissuade me. They mentioned that it would be foolhardy to go to a closed country where there was no freedom to preach the gospel. They advised that I go to a free area where I could witness without restraints, and then when Afghanistan opened I could go there to evangelize. I confessed that I did not know what God had in store, and like Peter all I could answer was that the Holy Spirit had told me to go.

7/AFTER YOU, MARCO POLO

Abraham obeyed. Away he went, not even knowing where he was going (Hebrews 11:8, TLB).

After sending in my application in the spring of 1947 for a teaching position in Afghanistan, I heard nothing for several months. I was so sure that God had called me to go there that I resigned as missionary secretary from Inter-Varsity. Because of the delay in hearing about my application, I made alternate plans to start on a Ph.D. program in Islamics at the University of Edinburgh in Scotland. This would give me further preparation for the work in Afghanistan. The very day I had sailed on the *Queen Elizabeth* for the British Isles, a letter came to my home from Washington, D.C., inviting me to come for a personal interview for the teaching position. After arriving in Scotland, I received this communication, which was forwarded to me there. I wrote back stating that I was taking further graduate studies but would be happy to interrupt them if I could get a teaching position in Afghanistan. An answer came back that they had plenty of applications; therefore they advised me to finish my degree and reapply later.

Along with my studies in Scotland, I was able to meet many other international students and found them hungry for friendship and open to hearing about the love of Jesus Christ. Having been helped by Dawson Trotman of the Navigators to appreciate the importance of discipling, I prayerfully selected seven students with whom I met individually an hour each week. Little did I then realize what God would do through their lives. They have become Christian leaders in their own countries. I was able to spend the spring term during 1948 at Cambridge University in England. There I met a young man who was a Muslim convert. He was having difficulty with the higher critical views of the Bible which he was being taught. We had rich times of fellowship together and he too by God's grace has become a Christian leader. Little did I realize then that he would become the Anglican Bishop of Iran. This whole experience of enrolling in education abroad opened my eyes to the great opportunity Christian students have to study *and witness* in universities all over the world.

The first Christian teachers-tentmakers to arrive in Afghanistan were Dick and Betty Soderberg. They had been contacted by Ralph Winter while Dick was a student at the newly established Fuller Theological Seminary. After their application to teach in Afghanistan had been accepted, Dick withdrew from his theological studies and he and Betty arrived in Kabul the winter of 1948.

In a real sense they followed in the tradition of Marco Polo, who in the thirteenth century had traveled through Afghanistan on his way to China. Even though he was a merchant by trade, he also was a self-supporting witness for Christ because he had as a motive for his journey the Christianization of these Asian areas.

The question naturally arises regarding the reason for Afghanistan remaining a closed country to the gospel. With the British Empire occupying the Indian subcontinent, the "great game" was to keep Russia, which was expanding in Central Asia, away from India's borders. Thus Afghanistan became the buffer between these two powers. For this reason, missionaries as well as business people and travelers were kept out of this no man's land. This policy of isolation fitted in with the desires of the freedom-loving Afghans who didn't want interference in their local politics or in their strong adherence to the Muslim religion. Even though missionaries had worked and prayed on the borders for many years, entrance for them to live, work, and witness in the land was continually denied.

Miss Flora Davidson, who came from a titled family in Scotland, worked for many years as an independent missionary on the northwest frontier of India. She wrote a book called *The Hidden Highway* in which she stated that by faith she knew that there eventually would be an entrance for the gospel into the closed land of Afghanistan, but as yet the way was not known. With the arrival of Dick and Betty Soderberg as teachers with the Afghan government, it suddenly became evident that the "hidden highway" was the new tentmaking ministry in that country. Just as Marco Polo had passed through Afghanistan almost seven centuries earlier as a merchant for Christ, so now self-supporting witnesses started entering the country again following the example and model of his tentmaking tradition. It was indeed an instance of "After you, Marco Polo."[1]

8/A WONDERFUL COUNTRY AHEAD

It is a wonderful country ahead, and the Lord loves us. He will bring us safely into the land and give it to us (Num. 14:7, 8, TLB).

I had told the Lord that I would be willing to be single all my life if that was what he wanted. But at the first Missionary Convention at the University of Toronto, I providentially met Betty Hutton of Hamilton, Ontario. She had grown up in a liberal church, but found Christ as her personal Savior while attending a Brethren conference. She had graduated from a teachers' college specializing in elementary education and was working with kindergarten children in a Canadian public school. As a member of the Teachers' Christian Fellowship, she was chosen to be their representative at the Missionary Convention. There, she heard Dr. Samuel Zwemer tell of the openings for work with children in Muslim nations. Because of her love for teaching boys and girls, she wanted to ask Dr. Zwemer more about these opportunities. Therefore she came to me and requested that I arrange an interview for her. For me, it was love at first sight. However, we both sought the Lord's will in the matter and became engaged two and a half years later. I then found out that she, too, had told the Lord that it if it were his will, she would serve him as a single person the rest of her life.

In the meantime, besides Dick and Betty Soderberg, other Christians had gone as teachers to Afghanistan. All these taught at Habibia College, which was the oldest secondary school in the country. Since Dick Soderberg had been an instructor in engineering at the University of Southern California, he quickly saw the need for a top-notch technical school in Afghanistan. He, therefore, drew up a proposal which he presented to the Ministry of Education. Consequently, on July 31, 1948, a contract was signed with the Government of Afghanistan. He was appointed director of the new school with the assignment to return to the States to recruit a faculty as well as to secure a library and equipment for the institute. The government agreed to give land for the new campus as well as to put up the necessary buildings. These were to be completed, the new faculty recruited, and the technical school opened by March of 1951. The Afghan government also paid for the transportation of the Soderberg family back to the States for this to be accomplished. The agreement received the approval of the Prime Minister as well as the Cabinet.

In the States, Dick Soderberg was able to set up a nonprofit corporation called "The Afghan Institute of Technology, Inc." This was administered by a Board of Directors which was headed up by Mr. Hugo Winter, a dedicated engineer in Los Angeles. Also, an article appeared in the *New York Times* (May 24, 1949) outlining the teaching opportunities in Afghanistan and mentioning the need for faculty. By early 1950 Dick Soderberg had lined up most of the teachers and had received contributions of thousands of dollars worth of texts and equipment for the new institute. The prospective faculty were all evangelical Christians who were qualified in their respective fields.

At this time, Dick Soderberg invited me to head up the English Teaching Department. I, therefore, studied linguistics and took courses at Columbia Teachers College in teaching English as a second language. Betty gave up her position in Canada and also enrolled at Biblical Seminary in New York City.

Living at the International House on Riverside Drive, I was able to get a weekly Bible study started there with students from various parts of the world. Permission for this had to be secured from the Director. Although at first he was opposed to it, he finally allowed this to take place and God worked in the hearts of the students there.

On weekends I pastored the small Presbyterian church in Palisades, New York, located on the beautiful west bank of the Hudson River. Each Sunday afternoon I also taught a Bible class on the Princeton University campus.

In June of 1950 Betty and I were married in Hamilton, Ontario, expecting to leave for Afghanistan at any time. But our departure was held up time after time. During the delay, God gave us a verse which greatly encouraged us. In our devotions we came across Numbers 14:8: "If the Lord delight in us, then he will bring us into this land, and give it us." We knew, as the Scriptures teach, that we were "accepted in the beloved." Therefore, we could rest assured that God delighted in us because Jesus Christ was our Savior. Thus in spite of postponements and disappointments, we believed that he would open the way into Afghanistan for the purpose of sharing the gospel with the people there.

While the delays dragged on, my mother diplomatically asked me what I would do if my bride one day said that she was hungry. It was well and good to plan to go to Afghanistan, but in the meantime I had assumed new responsibilities for which I should provide. Thus, I started looking for a temporary position. One evangelical church in Pennsylvania offered me the position of Pastor of Youth. However, they stipulated that the contract should be for at least two years. I told them that we believed God was calling us to Afghanistan and therefore I felt we should be free to leave whenever the way opened. They therefore withdrew the offer.

Dr. Herbert Mekeel of the First Presbyterian Church in Schenectady, New York, then invited Betty and me to come to assist with a new church which was being started in East Glenville. I mentioned to him about our desire to be free to be on call for Afghanistan. His reply was, "Whenever God opens the way for you to go to Afghanistan, then is when we want you to go! However, come and help us for a period of weeks or months, and then when God does open the way, you will have praying people from these churches behind you." Betty and I therefore spent eight happy months working there and getting to know dedicated Christian people who over the years have continued to back God's work in Afghanistan with prayer, gifts, and personnel.[1]

One cause for the delay was the fact that Dick Soderberg had not received word from the Afghan government which would enable him to return to negotiate all of the teachers' contracts as well as other matters. Therefore, those who had agreed to join the faculty met for a day of prayer and called on the Lord to overrule. God answered right after this. An air ticket was issued by the Afghan authorities in Washington D.C. for Dick Soderberg to return to Kabul. The rest of us then agreed to spend fifteen minutes a day praying just for him and the negotiations. The new contract was finally signed January 23, 1951. This opened the way for the faculty to go out and to start the new institution in March of 1951 as was previously planned.

However, while we were in the Schenectady area, a discouraging letter came from Dick Soderberg in Afghanistan. He mentioned that a nominal Christian American couple who were teaching at Habibia had heard that Betty and I planned to come out. They knew that my parents had served in Iran as missionaries and therefore they warned the Afghan officials that we might want to do the same there. With Islam's historical policy of forcibly converting conquered peoples, Afghan Muslims thought that Christian nations would do likewise. For this reason, they considered the British missionaries along their borders to be the religious branch of that empire's army. The term "missionary" to them had a political connotation. Dick Soderberg therefore went on to explain that our coming might jeopardize the whole project. He estimated it would take from three to five years for the authorities to forget what they had heard. He therefore reluctantly would have to get another person to fill the position for which I was slated. Once again, we took the matter to the Lord in prayer. In spite of the disappointment we trusted that he would fulfill his will. And we believed he had shown to us that in his good time he would bring us into the land and eventually allow it to be evangelized for Christ.

In March of 1951 Dr. Frank Laubach was invited to bring a literacy team to Afghanistan to help teach illiterates. A United Nations survey taken at that time revealed that 97 percent of the people there could not read or write. Formerly as a missionary in the Philippines, he had noted that many Christians in the churches were illiterate. If they were to grow spiritually and get jobs to help them economically, they needed to learn to read. He developed a simple system of relating letters of the alphabet with pictures which would start with the same symbol and sound. By association, people could then learn the alphabet of their language very quickly. Through this method he found that he could teach an illiterate to read his or her own language in two hours. His system has been applied to hundreds of languages and it has been estimated that through it over 100 million people have learned to read.

Dr. Laubach invited my father to join the team, since as a

missionary in Iran he had learned Persian, which was one of the two main languages spoken in Afghanistan. Others on the team were Mrs. Laubach, their son Dr. Robert Laubach, and an artist, Mr. Philip Gray. They were only in the country twenty-eight days. But during the first two weeks they produced six primers, three in Dari (the Persian dialect spoken in the country) and three in Pashtu. Then for the next fourteen days they demonstrated teaching methods to illiterate soldiers.

In gratitude for what Dr. Laubach had done, the King of Afghanistan awarded him with the highest honor ever granted to a foreigner. At the farewell reception the minister of education asked Dr. Laubach if he knew of any possible English teachers, since they needed more in the country. He mentioned that my father had a son who might be interested in coming. For this reason the minister got my name and address. I then received a cable inviting me to come to teach English at Habibia High School. Since this was right from the Afghan government, I would not jeopardize the position of others as could have happened had I gone out with the Afghan Institute of Technology.

While there, Dr. Laubach wrote, "A new group of engineers is just arriving in Kabul this month to set up an Afghan Technical College. All of these men and women in the employ of the Government of Afghanistan seemed to me the finest that America could send abroad."[2]

In spite of the tremendous difficulties involved in starting an institution at that time in Afghanistan, God wonderfully blessed and the Afghan Institute of Technology was a success right from the start. The whole faculty was made up of Christians who were well-qualified in their respective fields. Students who studied there either took up needed positions within the country or entered universities and vocational institutions for further training abroad. An article appeared in *Reader's Digest* telling the interesting story of the Afghan Institute of Technology.

But because the teachers were evangelicals, there was concern on the part of various American government officials. One embassy employee stated, "The Christians at the Afghan Institute of Technology are potentially a more dangerous threat here than the Russian Communists." What worried them was the fact that the presence of born-again believers in a strongly Muslim country might result in a violent reaction.

Without consulting the director or the faculty, the American government offered Afghanistan the assistance of taking over the funding and sponsorship of this school. Afghan officials were happy to have this project paid for by the United States since it would free their funds for other needs. Thus in 1955 the American State Department arranged for a contract with the University of Wyoming to supply teachers and to run the Afghan Institute of Technology.

All new teachers coming out under this imposed arrangement as well as those who wanted to renew had to sign a contract with the University of Wyoming which contained the following religious clause: "Employees are not to engage in religious proselytizing among citizens of Afghanistan and are to conduct themselves at all times in such a way as to reflect credit on the United States. The University will terminate the employment of any individual when it has been proved that such action is justified and necessary because of religious proselytizing. In the event of such termination the employee shall pay the cost of returning himself and family to the United States." When the constitutionality of this clause was questioned in the light of the basic American freedoms, a University of Wyoming official replied that it had been inserted at the insistence of the U.S. State Department. Also, the director of the American Aid Program openly announced after the takeover, "No more fundamentalists will be hired!"

In spite of such discrimination, several more Christian families applied and came out under the Wyoming team. The Afghan Institute of Technology has continued and now is part of the engineering branch of the University of Kabul. One indication that it was a success was seen when the Soviet Union also included in its aid to Afghanistan a multi-million dollar technical institute along with buildings, equipment, and faculty. Nevertheless, over a period of time all of the Christian teachers were gradually eased out. Many of them however joined other projects and stayed to work in Afghanistan under different auspices.

Mr. Hugo Winter, the former president of the Board of the Afghan Institute of Technology and the father of Paul Winter, who was the director in Kabul after Dick Soderberg, and of Ralph Winter, who helped start the work in Afghanistan, has written, "We must conclude that this project was eminently worthwhile, and we can only say, 'To God be the glory, great things he hath done.' "

9/HE WILL BRING US IN

Faithful is he that calleth you, who also will do it (1 Thes. 5:24).

After my father returned from Afghanistan where he had served
with the Laubach literacy team, he accompanied me to
Washington, D.C. to speak with the Afghan ambassador about the
offer I had received to teach there. I felt it only right to mention
before I signed the contract that I was a Christian minister. This
then would avoid the accusation that I had secured the position
under false pretenses. He stated that since I had the teaching
qualifications, this would be quite all right. He further mentioned
that most of the teachers in Afghanistan were Muslim priests and
added that it would also be good to have a Christian priest
teaching their young people.

The text of the contract stated that I would agree not to
interfere in politics, business, or religion. I asked the Afghan
ambassador for a clarification of this. If a student asked me a
religious question, would I be free to answer him or not? His
Excellency stated that as a teacher it was my responsibility to
answer students' questions. He added that this clause had been
put in the contract to try to avoid incidents such as had occurred
when representatives from the heretical Muslim Ahmadiyya Sect
had preached their doctrines in the streets in Afghanistan and had
caused riots. I thanked him for this clarification and therefore
signed the contract.

Four days before Betty and I were scheduled to leave, I
received a person-to-person phone call from the Afghanistan

embassy in Washington. An official there stated that the ambassador wanted to see me again the next day. I mentioned that we had planned to go into New York at that time to ship books and things by surface since we were to take off shortly for Afghanistan. He said, "We are not sure that you are going after all!" I asked him the reason, since the contract had already been signed by both parties. He stated that he could not discuss the matter on the phone, but that I would have to see the ambassador again.

That night we telephoned many praying friends, telling them we did not know what the problem was, but asking them to make it a matter of earnest intercession. We had already had a commissioning service at the First Presbyterian Church in Schenectady, had said farewell to friends, and my wife's parents had come from Canada to see us off. Now it seemed that it was going to end in a disappointing anticlimax.

My father graciously agreed to go to New York to ship our things surface while Betty's parents drove us to Washington. At the meeting with the Afghan ambassador, he said that he wanted to be sure that I understood the religious situation in their nation. I told him that having grown up in the adjacent area of Iran, I was acquainted with a similar Islamic country. I further mentioned my desire was to help his nation and his people and I did not want to cause trouble. He then said that with this clarification, he was happy I was going. Disappearing for a few minutes, he returned with a dozen new Arrow shirts which he asked me to take to the prime minister in Afghanistan. Even though we already had our limit in weight, I could not refuse. I was grateful to God for this evidence of our acceptance.

I had applied for a renewal of my U.S. passport some weeks before, but as yet had not received it. Since our departure date was so near and we were in Washington, I thought I would stop by the State Department to see if they might have sent it to the wrong address. But when they found out who I was, they ushered me in to see the head of the passport division. The first question asked me was, "Are you going to Afghanistan to preach the gospel?" I answered that I realized this country as yet did not have religious freedom, but I believed God was going to open it eventually and when he did, it would be a privilege to witness for my Lord. The director then said, "This is what we have been afraid of!" I was then sent to different offices in the State

Department where they tried to dissuade me from going to Afghanistan, saying that it would be very foolish for a Christian minister to be in that country which was so religiously and politically sensitive, located on the border of Russia and China. They asked what the attitude of the Afghan ambassador had been to my going. I told them that I had just talked with him and that he said it was all right. Since only those who advocate the forceful overthrow of our government can be refused a passport, they finally and reluctantly gave me mine.

It was only after I got to Afghanistan that one of the diplomats there who had been serving in the Washington embassy explained what had happened. He said that when I applied for my passport, a CIA security check was run on me and they found out that I was an ordained minister. The State Department therefore advised the Afghan embassy to cancel my contract, stating that I would be a dangerous person to have in that area. And then the Afghan diplomat added as he displayed their delightful independent spirit, "But we did not listen to the State Department!"

Betty and I thankfully took off as scheduled with Pan American from New York on June 25, 1951. Since no plane service had yet been started into Afghanistan, we flew to Pakistan. On arriving in Peshawar, I inquired about means of travel overland through the Khyber Pass to Kabul. The only regular transportation was in a truck which had been redesigned into a bus with hard wooden seats. Since we were expecting our first child in a few months, it would be foolish to try to travel in this way. A taxi driver said that he would take us, but he wanted over $200 for the 180-mile trip. He said the road was so rough that he would need to repair his car after the journey. We didn't have that much money and therefore committed the matter to the Lord in prayer.

As we were eating supper in the Dean's Hotel, a man came to our table and called me by name. I wondered whether Washington had traced me there already. He said that there was a new Chevrolet station wagon with a chauffeur ready to drive us to Kabul the next morning. After dinner I asked the hotel manager who this person was. He then asked me if I were not a United Nations expert. When I told him that I was not, he said that this gentleman had just completed his tour of duty with the U.N. in Afghanistan and was on his way home. Upon arriving at the hotel he had asked the manager whether any United Nations experts had arrived and the manager thought I was one. I went to the gentleman's room and explained that we were not with the United Nations. He was surprised to hear this, but then graciously said that the car was going back anyway and therefore we were welcome to go with it.

Even though we started early the next morning and drove through the Khyber Pass, it was almost midnight before we reached Kabul. The hotel there was already closed. The chauffeur knocked on the door, which was finally opened and we were shown to a room. The sheets on the beds had obviously been used since there were blood marks where former occupants had killed mosquitos. There was a high incidence of malaria in the city, and approximately half of those who came to Afghanistan contracted this illness. Betty turned to me and said, "We can't stay here. We must go to another hotel!" I had to reply, "This is the only one there is."

The next day a Christian couple invited us to stay with them until we could rent a place of our own. Furthermore, I had to start teaching right away since my salary did not begin until I was actually working. I thus began to teach English to 150 students at Habibia High School. There was warm appreciation and acceptance by the students. They have a saying that your teacher is your second father. Another Christian teacher and I met each morning and prayed over the lists of our students. Even though we did not have the liberty to share Christ with them openly, we did have freedom to pray for them.

It had now been over four years since I first applied to go to Afghanistan. During the delays God had encouraged us with the words in Numbers 14:8, "If the Lord delight in us, then he will bring us into this land, and give it us." He had been faithful in enabling us to get into the country, but we realized that this was just the beginning. God gave us the privilege of living in Afghanistan over twenty-one years until 1973. The first four-and-a-half years I taught as an employee of the Afghan government, and later permission was granted me to be a chaplain to the international community there. We discovered through experience that God "is able to do exceeding abundantly above all that we ask or think" (Ephesians 3:20).

10/TENTMAKERS TODAY

Whatever you do, do it all for the glory of God (1 Cor. 10:31, NIV).

The following are short sketches about recent or current tentmakers we have known or about whom we have heard. Their number could be multiplied many times over. But these are given as illustrations of what tentmakers are doing around the world today.

AN ARMY DOCTOR

Dr. Arthur Iliff had been a medical missionary from Britain on the northwest frontier of India before World War II. He had longed to get into the closed area of Waziristan but was denied permission. However, during the war he was made a medical officer in the British army and was assigned to thousands of Pathan soldiers in Waziristan. Of this experience he wrote, "Though the color of my shirt may have temporarily changed, beneath it my thoughts, hopes, and aims remain the same. I can see God's hand in it all and thank him that he has given me this chance of preparing the way for missionary advance."[1]

A MENNONITE ENGLISH TEACHER

In Central Asia I met a young man who looked completely out of context. At first I thought he was a Jewish rabbi. He had a beard and was wearing a black hat and suit. He told me his name was James Lowry, that he was a Mennonite from Ohio, and that he was teaching English in a government high school in the state of Swat in northern Pakistan. He and his wife had been able to have Swati students in their home there and were studying the Bible with these young men who had never seen the Christian Scriptures before. Since I knew that Swat was an Islamic area closed to missions, I asked him how he and his wife had been able to get in. He replied, "I never heard of the place! I applied under a Fulbright fellowship to teach English in Germany and was sent to Swat!" Meeting this Christian friend was a further indication to me of what the Spirit of God is doing today by getting the gospel into closed areas through tentmakers.

A CHRISTIAN ENGINEER

Another Christian couple working in Central Asia as tentmakers have had a rich ministry. The husband, an engineer, received over twice the salary he would have had in the United States. He and his wife were thus able to give over half of their income to missions. Furthermore, they conducted Bible studies in their home, were active in the local expatriate congregation, led nationals to Christ, and built them up in their faith.

AN EMBASSY SECRETARY

Ruby Herboldt came to Afghanistan in 1958 as a secretary with the American embassy. When she landed at the Kabul Airport she prayed, "Lord, I give these two future years to you. I know that I am weak and vulnerable, but I believe you have brought me here and I trust you to keep me pure, faithful, and serviceable for you." When different ones in the embassy found out that she did not swear, drink, or smoke, they said they would give her one week and she would be carousing like the rest of them. She was housed with two other secretaries. One of them told her that liquor was a big thing in embassy life and she would be expected to pay her share of what they served in the house. This bothered her, but at first she said nothing. When the opportunity arose, she mentioned her concern to one of the other secretaries. She reassured her by saying, "If you have convictions and qualms about it, there is no reason why we can't change the bookkeeping system and keep the liquor and groceries separate." She volunteered to teach a Sunday school class, was faithful in attending church services, and participated in early morning prayer meetings before her job would begin. She carried on an effective tentmaking testimony in a difficult environment. She finished her two-year assignment as a bright, victorious believer and God gave her a wonderful Christian husband, Vern Isaac, another tentmaker working with the State Department whom she first met in Afghanistan.

A MEDICAL COUPLE

Traveling as a young man, Dr. Robert Shaw had peered into Afghanistan from the Khyber Pass in 1929. He had hoped to be a medical missionary and work on the borders until the opportunity opened up to enter. However, in medical school he contracted tuberculosis which left a spot on his lung and disqualified him from acceptance by a mission board. He then specialized in thoracic surgery and taught medicine in Dallas, Texas. But he still had hopes that some day he might serve in Afghanistan. Therefore in 1961 when Care Medico invited him to head up their team in Kabul, he readily accepted. Along with his wife Ruth, a registered nurse, he was able to help the Afghan people greatly. He performed the first open heart surgery in the country.

After his first tour in Afghanistan, he returned to Dallas and was working at the Parkland Hospital where President Kennedy and Governor Connally were taken after they were shot. He was called in on the President's case and was the surgeon in charge of Governor Connally's operation. He also was assigned to examine Oswald after he was shot. Thus unexpectedly he found himself at the center of this historic and tragic drama.

He and his wife returned again to Afghanistan in 1966 to set up a special chest surgery unit and worked there until 1968. In 1970 they were invited to Afghanistan again where he served as a professor in the Nangrahar University Medical School at

Jalalabad, fifty miles west of the Khyber Pass. Dr. Shaw's father, a Methodist minister, had said, "What the world needs today is dedicated Christian laymen." Dr. Shaw adds, "Although I still feel that being a minister or missionary is the greatest calling, I believe my father's statement was correct. And person-to-person contact in deeds of understanding is the manner in which laymen can make their greatest impact. God has a job for every individual."

A TEACHER OF THE BLIND

Kathleen Stewart came to Afghanistan October 28, 1967, to help teach blind children. She served under the auspices of The Evangelical Alliance Mission (TEAM) and raised her own support by selling her farm and livestock in the States. Her training had been in the area of educating the handicapped, and she was effective in teaching blind Afghan boys and girls. In spite of dreadful difficulties, she always had a joyous and victorious spirit. In October 1968 the home in which she and another teacher of the blind were living burned down, but no one was hurt. Later concern for her health due to cancer forced her to return to the States. After a painful illness, she went to be with the Lord in January of 1970. As a tentmaker for Christ, she took the investment of her farm with her on high, even as her Lord had said, "Lay up for yourselves treasures in heaven" (Matthew 6:20).

THE PRINCE OF PEACE CORPS

Christians have also served with the Peace Corps and similar programs sponsored by various nations. Even though their pay has been minimal, they have been self-supporting witnesses or tentmakers. Some jokingly referred to the Peace Corps as "a second Children's Crusade." But then when various critics saw what was accomplished by many of these volunteers, one writer stated: "With the creation of the Peace Corps . . . it became obvious that the tremendous idealism of the young people could be harnessed as a positive force for society."[2] Christian volunteers had an added motivation as members of "the Prince of Peace Corps." We had the joy of meeting and knowing some of them in Afghanistan and we thank God for each one.

AN AIR FORCE COLONEL

When Russia and China became atomic powers, America
established an air base in Peshawar, Pakistan, to monitor
thermonuclear explosions. It was from this base that Francis
Powers took off on his U-2 flight over Russia. The head of this air
base for some time was Colonel Ridge Ryan, a dedicated man of
God. Not only was he a tentmaker for Christ in this sensitive
position, but since retiring from the Air Force he has become
pastor of a church in Southern California.

A NURSE

A former missionary nurse married a Christian engineer working
in Tehran, Iran. "People now ask me why I gave up being a
missionary," she states. "I say that I have not. Christian lay
people are needed abroad even as they are at home. I have just as
much a call to be a self-supporting witness as I had when I was a
church-supported missionary."

A CHRISTIAN LAWYER

Another former American missionary is now serving as a
Christian lawyer in a Middle Eastern country. He has even taken
out citizenship there and is married to a Christian national. His
witness is more effective than ever.[3]

AN OIL ENGINEER

Bob Old and his wife, Jimmie, have served with oil companies in
Venezuela and Iran. Not only has Bob done an outstanding job as
a petroleum engineer from Texas, but he and his wife have carried
on an effective witness for Jesus Christ.

"My aims and desires were for professional and worldly
success," Bob writes about his early life. "I achieved my goal and
found no fulfillment, no peace of heart or mind, no joy—not even
happiness. I had left God . . . and had lost my wife and children,
even though we were still living together. God knew how to get
my attention! In his love and mercy he brought me to
near-bankruptcy and put a hunger in my heart for him." At the

same time his wife, Jimmie, also came back to the Lord and they both now testify, "We knew God had forgiven each of us and that we were truly cleansed of all unrighteousness through his blood, but it was a long hard road forgiving each other and ourselves and really accepting God's forgiveness. The making of restitution for our sins against others was hard, but God's grace was more than sufficient! By his Spirit he brought to light all that needed to be made right with others. He led us to strong mature Christians who could teach us from his Word as well as from their lives. He baptized us in the Holy Spirit and he brought us to a place in our walk with him that he could minister through us to others. Having drunk deeply of all the world has to offer, we can identify with those walking in darkness. We can truly say, 'There, but for the grace of God, go I.' Perhaps for this reason, he gave us a counseling ministry that began during our last years in Iran. We have seen God change sin-sick, confused, lost lives just as dramatically as he changed ours."

Working with the National Iranian Oil Company, Bob did such an outstanding job technically that his work will save that country billions of dollars worth of petroleum. He devised a system whereby much more oil could be retrieved from wells by pumping natural gas into them when they ran dry. This forced the remaining petroleum out of sandstone deposits, making it possible to pump much more from the wells. Furthermore, the natural gas also can be retrieved before the empty cavarans are filled with sea water.

Bob also spent his spare time in Tehran preaching and leading Christian life seminars. He and his wife had a constant flow of visitors coming to their apartment who were in need of prayer, healing, and counsel.

A CATTLE RAISER
AND A GOVERNMENT TEACHER

A missionary from Zambia in Africa states that the most effective Christian he had met there was a self-supporting witness involved in cattle raising. Another tentmaker who teaches mathematics in that same country writes, "Being a government employee carries with it the advantage of having a clean slate. We have no label but 'Christian.' "

AN EDUCATOR

Ruth Siemens has devoted herself to a tentmaking ministry in education overseas for twenty years. She has also been used by God to help out Inter-Varsity movements in Peru, Brazil, Portugal, and Spain. She is now involved in counseling potential tentmakers through her organization Global Opportunities.

A MINING ENGINEERING COUPLE

Cathy Phelps, who was a former Inter-Varsity staff worker, went with her husband, Barry, who is a mining engineer, to Bolivia, Colombia, and Surinam in Latin America. She was so thrilled with this experience that to help others undertaking a similar ministry she has written a book, *The Guide to Moving Overseas*.[4]

These are but a few examples of the many self-supporting witnesses for Christ around the world. We have also met other committed Christians overseas in international business, in professions, in secretarial positions, in medical work as doctors and nurses, in military service, in development programs, in teaching positions, in research projects, in foreign universities as students, in the Peace Corps, in the United Nations, in the diplomatic service, and those who are tourists. These are Christians who have served in tentmaking capacities overseas. But they need assistance and encouragement if their witness is to be effective.

11/TENTMAKING MAKES SENSE

In your thinking be mature (1 Cor. 14:20, NASB).

"One of the most significant manifestations of the work of the
Holy Spirit in the world today," writes Dr. Clyde Taylor, who
headed the National Association of Evangelicals, "is the leadership
he is giving in turning the members of the church back to lay
evangelism, to the methods that prevailed during the apostolic
era."[1] Just as with the Reformation there was a renewed
realization of the scriptural revelation of "the priesthood of the
believers," so today many are appreciating once again the truth of
the evangelistic mission of all Christians. The Bible speaks of him
who has made us "kings and priests unto God," but also records
how Christ commanded all of us to evangelize the world (Mark
16:15). The basic difference is that Christians who are
fully-supported leave their nets and follow Christ, whereas those
who are self-supporting take their nets with them and follow him.

The difficulty arises with the false dichotomy between
fully-supported missionaries and tentmakers. There is often the
same misconception in the division between the clergy and the
laity. Reflecting on this problem, Dr. Ross Kinsler writes,

The churches urgently need to engage their most capable leaders
—most of whom are not pastors and therefore have never taken
seriously God's call to them. These leaders, who are deeply
involved in the economic, social, and political structures and who
represent every profession and field of knowledge, must be

challenged to work out the meaning of the gospel in today's world. Believers can now be found in every society and subculture and they are all essential for the church's missionary encounter with the world.[2]

The church needs to regain the vision that every Christian is a witness at home and abroad.

A dedicated nurse told me that she had an offer to serve in a secular hospital abroad, but that she had a guilty conscience about accepting this position since she did not feel it was spiritual service. She then recounted the outstanding opportunities for witness she was having in a secular hospital here at home. In regard to this misconception, Sir Kenneth Grubb observes:

At home we encourage our laymen in evangelization, but abroad we illogically think of evangelization as a special vocation. The words "every Christian a missionary" are frequently on our lips, yet when we lift up our eyes and look on the harvest fields of the world we have a different method in mind for their evangelization. We think of the special vocation as different from everyday faithful Christian witness. There is something illogical here. Yet among those who man the offices of trading companies and who sell goods, how few are bearing an effective Christian witness. The missionary enterprise remains outside the industrial invasion. There are positions abroad satisfactorily paid in every respect which are being filled by godless men and women while Christians of equal qualifications are content to remain at home.[3]

Not only is it logical for lay Christians to share the gospel around the world, but this also affords a model for national believers to follow. Dr. John Nevius, a missionary to China who influenced the Lord's work in Korea with his missiological strategy, taught that each Christian should "abide in the calling wherein he was found," support himself by his own work, and be a witness for Christ by his life and word in his own neighborhood.[4] This principle was put into practice in the church in Korea and has resulted in vitality and growth.

Roland Allen, who also was a missionary to China, had clear insight into the importance of tentmakers. He wrote that there was no other way to accomplish world evangelization than to find men and women who had a strong and deep missionary spirit and to urge them to go as unofficial missionaries.[5] He clearly saw the importance in having Christians from professional ranks go to other countries, support themselves, and propagate the gospel. He observed that most Christians who go to other shores never think of themselves as missionaries responsible for carrying the good news. He states that this results from the fact that missions are viewed as exclusively the job of special agents sent out by mission boards.[6] Sir Kenneth Grubb echoes the same concern.

Laity should not leave the Christian witness to the specialist. For the people of Asia, Africa and Latin America cannot be reached for Christ by ministers alone. Lay men and women of these continents hold positions of leadership and responsibility. They can often be helped best by other laymen who have themselves wrestled in the long struggle to interpret the meaning of the faith in the complex structure of modern life.[7]

Just as Christian lay people form such a vital part of the local congregation at home, so they can play a decisive role in witness on the international scene.

Dr. Hendrik Kraemer, a brilliant scholar from Holland who served for many years as an evangelistic missionary in Indonesia, grapples with this problem in his book *A Theology of Laity*. He observed, "The lay-membership of the Church has never enjoyed the distinction of being treated with care and thoroughness as a matter of specific theological importance or significance. This is an inexcusable lack and an indication of a partly misoriented understanding of the Church in its wholeness." Dr. Kraemer points out that throughout most of history the laity has existed as "frozen credit."[8] He goes on to underline the fact that "the ministry of *diakonia* of the Church applies to all its members."[9] He notes a beginning of a change in Christian thinking regarding this. "Churches, rediscovering their missionary obligation and suddenly becoming aware of the hugeness of the task, turn to the laity with the argument that every Christian is a witness and/or a missionary."[10] He adds, "In ever-increasing missionary activity, the laity has found an outlet for its gifts and participation in the missionary task of the Church in the world, the call for the lay apostolate."[11]

THE TWO TYPES OF TENTMAKERS

"Christians working overseas may be divided into two broad categories," writes Dr. Howard Mattsson-Boze, who himself taught in Tehran as a self-supporting witness, "those whose primary motivation is Christian witnessing; and those who have a primary commitment to their occupation or discipline, seeking to work it out as a Christian."[12] The first type, like the Apostle Paul, are principally motivated to go overseas to be witnesses for Jesus Christ, and their job is a means to this end. The second category are those who may suddenly find themselves assigned abroad by their company without having planned to go as a self-supporting missionary. Both types can render great service to the Lord.

DISADVANTAGES TO TENTMAKING

Some recent writers have described the disadvantages of tentmaking in such a way that many have been discouraged from attempting this type of witness. There are limitations and problems; yet these should not rob us of a God-given means which can supplement the ministry of regular missionaries to accomplish the evangelization of the world. The following are problem areas which should be kept in mind:

1) The agency with which a Christian is working may seek to curtail one's testimony and limit religious freedom. But these difficulties also exist in secular positions at home.

2) Tentmaking usually involves a full-time job and therefore makes it difficult to find time to master the local language. The greatest need abroad is for cross-cultural witness, which requires a good grasp of the language. But some tentmakers have mastered the language of the area where they work and thus have increased both their effectiveness on the job and their witness.

3) The term of service for a tentmaker is usually limited to one or two years. This makes it difficult to learn the language and to make lasting contributions to the growth of the church. But many contracts are renewable, especially when a person has done a good job. Some tentmakers, after completing their service with a secular organization, have returned as missionaries under a regular board.

4) The job demands on one's time may appear to limit the opportunity for witness. But a Christian can usually witness by life and word while on duty when this is done discreetly. Even a

church-supported missionary doctor or nurse who carries a heavy load of work must learn to witness both on and off the job.

5) Some self-supporting witnesses have been accused of being deceptive because they are "missionaries in disguise." An accusation like this gives an opportunity for a Christian to point out that secularists are missionaries of materialism. All represent what they believe.

6) Another criticism is that Christian tentmakers have a double motive, that of being loyal to their employer but also to their faith. In answering this, one can reply with Christ that people are to render to Caesar the things that are Caesar's, but to God the things that are God's.

7) Another disadvantage is that often tentmakers do not have people in their home churches praying for them the way regular missionaries do. And yet by careful effort, self-supporting witnesses can also get a faithful group of Christian friends backing them regularly in prayer.

8) Many companies which have a large contingent of foreigners working in a particular nation often segregate them in special compounds. Almost all of their contacts are with people from their own country and associations with nationals and the local Christians are limited. This too can be a disadvantage. But by concerted effort one can usually overcome this and meaningful contacts with local people can be established.

9) Another disadvantage is that many organizations frown on the sharing of one's faith openly with local nationals. Most of these have a considerable investment in the country where they are working and therefore fear any kind of incident which might provoke the ill-will of the host nation and possibly lead to restrictions or even expropriation. Christians need to be discreet in regard to the legitimate interests of the organization which they serve. In areas where religious liberty is restricted, the Lord's servants need to be "wise as serpents, and harmless as doves."

10) Another disadvantage is the fact that tentmakers usually do not have the opportunity that regular missionaries do of taking orientation before working in a foreign nation. Some are assigned by their company to another country and only have a short time to get ready. Many are flown into strange environments with little if any preparation. Organizations are finding out that it is to their own interest to give proper orientation. Without this, not only is the efficiency of their employees impaired, but also many of them

are unable to adjust, and they resign from their positions. It is vital for tentmakers to get as much orientation as possible.

11) There is the real danger that tentmakers can get so overwhelmed in their work that they cannot witness. Watchman Nee, the great Chinese Christian, discovered this from personal experience. In 1942 he took on the directorship of a pharmaceutical factory to try to be self-supporting even as the Apostle Paul was. However, he became so ensnared by business responsibilities that for five years he had to stop preaching. In 1947 he publicly confessed his error in becoming involved with the factory and handed it over to the Christian congregation in Shanghai.[13]

12) Another practical disadvantage a tentmaker often has is the lack of spiritual accountability. Peter Wagner mentions that for a fully-supported worker, dependence can be a good thing. It keeps the home churches on their knees and the missionaries on their toes.[14] Tentmaker association with mission agencies helps this.

13) A further danger for a tentmaker is that of serving alone in an area without Christian fellowship. To avoid this, it would be best to go along with other believers as a team for mutual encouragement and help. Our Lord sent his disciples two by two, and the Holy Spirit called both Barnabas and Paul.

ADVANTAGES TO TENTMAKING

From his experience as a tentmaker in Tehran, Dr. Howard Mattsson-Boze lists the following advantages to this type of ministry:

Such persons are not identified as clergymen or as paid propagandists for their religion.

In the course of their work, they often meet classes of people who missionaries usually do not reach: professional men and women, educated persons, factory workers, university professors.

They often have more money than regular missionaries, receiving in many cases quite a comfortable salary from the government or their company, although there are exceptions.

They are of little or no cost to the Christian Church, either at home or abroad.

They have satisfactions of their own professional accomplishment which may balance the frustrations and discouragements which may arise in the course of Christian witness in different areas (such as many Muslim lands).

They are free to respond to needs which may not be in the program of a mission.[15]

Herbert Kane mentions other advantages. He observes that tentmakers have access to countries which are closed to regular missionaries.[16] He points out that it is imperative for the Christian church to seek ways of getting the gospel to the ends of the earth, and therefore this approach is essential for entering areas where fully-supported missionaries are not allowed.[17]

Another advantage he mentions is that "in the eyes of the host country, he is a secular person with a secular calling and anything he does contributes directly or indirectly to nation building." He further points out that a tentmaker "is free from the stigma of proselytizing."[18]

One tentmaker working with a mission as a field partner has written in a strategy paper, "Those who work alongside nationals of a host country in industrial and government positions often have ideal opportunities. Their relationship with nationals can provide a very natural setting for sharing the Gospel."[19] This highlights the fact that not only do geographic areas need a witness for Christ, but also business groups, government circles, military personnel, and many other mosaics of society exist where lay Christians can minister. Dr. Donald McGavran has pointed out the importance of witnessing within a homogeneous unit.[20] Thus workers in the same profession have the *entree* with others in the same occupation.

THE OBLIGATION
OF CHRISTIAN TENTMAKERS TO WITNESS

Dr. Theodore Pennell of Bannu, on the border of Afghanistan, who early in this century gave his life as a Christian physician working on the northwest frontier, wrote, "Every Christian, be he in civil or military service, in trade or in profession or merely a temporary visitant can and should be doing Christian missionary work."[21] Another Christian physician, Dr. Agnes Clausen, from Denmark, who was able to visit in Afghanistan during 1924, anticipated the work tentmakers could do when she wrote:

The day has already come when Afghanistan is open for the Christian professional. What Afghanistan needs at this time is 'the children of the Kingdom' in many different positions; clever, pious, meek, lowly, self-denying people, men and women with great love which hopes all, believes all, and endures all. I do not mean missionaries in the usual understanding of the word. We have for many years been praying that the doors of Afghanistan may be opened. Let us change our prayer and pray for the right men and women to enter the doors which are already open.[22]

Although the market for pastors in suburban American churches is saturated, nevertheless the needs for Christian workers are great in inner city areas as well as abroad. Of the 2.7 billion unreached people identified by the Lausanne Congress for World Evangelization in 1974,[23] only 1 percent are in the United States and Canada. Ninety-nine percent of the unreached live in the rest of the world. For example, even though half of the people of the world live on the continent of Asia, less than 2 percent of these call themselves Christians.

Dr. Ralph Winter of the U.S. Center for World Mission states that in order to reach the unreached in Africa and Asia, we will need 100 times the number of missionaries which we are now sending.[24] It is through tentmakers, along with regular missionaries, that such a number realistically could be engaged.

Another advantage tentmakers have is that if they are taking jobs needed and approved by the host country, they usually have no difficulty securing visas. In many areas this is proving more and more a problem to regular missionaries. Also, during the times of inflation, when it costs so much to support missionaries fully, encouraging tentmakers is a way of securing additional financial assistance to meet the need for more workers. Self-supporting witnesses not only relieve churches of the need of paying for their expenses, but they themselves often can be of great assistance in financially backing regular missionaries.

Employment abroad has potential for good and for evil. In Afghanistan a Westerner who was a nominal Christian had an Afghan neighbor call on him. He became very nervous when his Muslim friend mentioned that he had become a Christian, because at that time in Afghanistan apostasy from Islam was a crime punishable by death. He asked him what he meant by this. The man replied, "I drink whiskey now too. Do you have any you can give me?" He had seen this expatriate drunk and to him, becoming a Christian meant leaving the prohibition of Islam and having the license to drink liquor. In areas abroad one can hear nationals swearing in the name of our Lord Jesus Christ, people who have never had a chance to hear the meaning of the gospel. They have learned to curse from nominal Christians. As the book *The Overseas American* states, "The failure of the Church to substantiate the claim that Christianity is the faith for the world is due to the fact that the multitudes of Asia and Africa have failed to see in the lives of those who have come to them from the Christian West any compelling reason why they should forsake their own spiritual and moral values for those of Christianity."[25] Dr. William Danker notes, "It is not difficult to understand the Third World's fear of economic neocolonialism. There is room for Christian businessmen who will organize economic enterprises for the benefit of indigenous people and of indigenous Christian churches." Dr. Danker also points out that when the Mennonite and Basel Missions assisted the local people with employment in business projects, "economic activities proved to be the base and nucleus of the largest and strongest congregations in both groups."[26]

It is no longer a matter of whether tentmaking witness around the world is justified or not. It is here. The question is, Are born again Christians going to take full advantage of it or are they going to allow nominal Christians to use these self-supporting positions as hindrances rather than helps to the spread of the gospel?

12/TENTMAKING
STUDENTS ABROAD

They that were scattered abroad went every where preaching the word (Acts 8:4).

If Arabs in the Muslim world are to be reached, "something new has to be done," says Bruce Bell, a former missionary. "My crazy idea would be to recruit young Christians who would be willing to go to the universities of the Arab world to get their degrees. These would be committed, Bible-trained young people who would live Spirit-filled lives, identifying with the Arabs in every possible way and making friends. A student after two years ought to have 400 friends. The people are amazingly hospitable. The idea is that the Christian's life is so different that the people are going to begin to ask questions. There is nothing in the law against sharing your faith that way."[1] This is not only an effective way for reaching the Arab nations but also the whole world for Christ. The educational institutions of the nations afford a key opportunity for evangelism.

Bill Bright of Campus Crusade has said, "Students represent a major source of manpower to help change the course of history. They need to be reached for Christ."[2] If 10,000 mature born again students could enroll in universities overseas, with replacements taking their places every couple of years, this would do much to evangelize the world for Christ. Undergraduates are freer than any other group when it comes to witnessing in Communist and Muslim nations which are usually closed to traditional missions. Students all over the world have a reputation for espousing far-out ideas and therefore even their gospel witness is often overlooked.

Dr. Waldron Scott of the World Evangelical Fellowship states, "Everywhere I go, students are deeply concerned about how they can carry out a witness for Jesus Christ as laymen serving abroad."[3] One of the most strategic ways in which these young people can witness is by enrolling in universities around the world. Professor Herbert Kane mentions that students have distinct advantages in that "being young they are able to identify with the youth of the host countries, adapt to their customs, and respond to their needs."[4]

Communists are sending students who have been indoctrinated into universities all around the world, and this accounts for the fact that Marxism has gained such a strong foothold in so many institutions of higher learning from Tokyo to Rio de Janeiro. Moreover, Muslim students from oil-rich nations have established their Islamic associations on campuses throughout Western countries and are not hesitant to share their faith with others. The published purpose of the Muslim Students' Association of the United States and Canada is to help "every truth seeker to know the Islamic message and recruit, train, and mobilize Muslim workers to use all appropriate opportunities to propagate Islam." Of their membership 38 percent are on student visas, 30 percent are immigrants, and 32 percent are naturalized citizens of the U.S. and Canada. Of these, 37 percent are undergraduates, 47 percent are engaged in graduate studies, and 16 percent are faculty or staff members of academic institutions.[5] The Muslim Students' Association lists the names and addresses of 310 mosques and Islamic organizations in North America.[6]

FEASIBILITY

Christians who have studied abroad have found it not only to be a rich educational and cultural experience, but also an outstanding opportunity to witness for Christ. Dr. Mark Hanna went from the States to the American University of Beirut for his undergraduate work. He roomed with Muslim students from Saudi Arabia and Turkey. Another Christian and he met regularly to pray for the whole faculty and student body. During his final year there he was able to have evangelistic meetings to which hundreds of students came, of whom nearly 200 made decisions to accept Jesus Christ as Savior.

Another Christian student is taking his Ph.D. at a North

African university in a nation where missionaries are not allowed. He is active in an expatriate Christian congregation and also is quietly in fellowship with some national believers. Along with his education he is engaged in effective evangelism.

Alice Winters took a year's study at Seminario Biblico in San Jose, Costa Rica, where she also mastered Spanish. She had an effective ministry with Christian students in the seminary as well as with non-Christians in the secular university. She now has returned to Latin America as a fully supported missionary and has special acceptance because of having been a student in institutions there.

One Christian decided to enroll at Tehran University. He then stayed on there as an engineer and businessman. He and his wife not only worked with national Christians and churches, but have also assisted many missionaries and other expatriates. Furthermore, they helped establish a Christian school for children from both the international and the national communities. As tentmakers in a predominantly Islamic environment, they faced many difficulties. And yet God has used them. They have seen many friends come to a saving knowledge of Jesus Christ.

Another, even though he already had two Master's degrees, entered a university in a closed country as an undergraduate. On a student visa he and his wife have been able to lead Muslims to Christ, carry them on in their faith, and get them associated with other national believers. They have also supervised Scripture translation, Christian literature distribution, and the preparation of radio programs to be broadcast back into that country.

OPPORTUNITY

Countries all over the world, including Communist China, are sending students to Western nations, and therefore on a reciprocal basis they stand ready to receive into their institutions of higher learning those who want to study. Many of them are also able to give scholarship assistance. Except for the cost of transportation, education in these countries usually is more financially reasonable than it would be in the West.

Study abroad provides an opportunity to master languages where they are spoken. Students can also engage in linguistic research, reduce oral tongues to written alphabets, produce dictionaries, prepare descriptive grammars, and translate the Scriptures.

Other areas of study and research can be: the local culture, the history of the country, literature, anthropology, art, archaeology, and medicine. Many secular students who have not been able to get into medical schools in North America are taking this training abroad. The Institute of International Education reported that during the academic year 1975–76 there were 50,000 U.S. students studying abroad, which was a rise of 40 percent over the figure twenty years earlier.[7]

STRATEGY

If Christian students are to be effective in their ministry abroad, proper planning and careful preparation is important. Our Lord sent out his disciples two by two. It is far better for those who enroll in educational institutions around the world to do so as a team of two or more Christians together.

Orientation for students going abroad is also an important part of their preparation. Missionary Internship has some very fine programs. This is an evangelical, interdenominational service agency which provides pre-service training for mission-related personnel. (See address of this and other agencies at back of book.)

Another vital matter is that of securing intercessory backing. This can be done through local churches, prayer meetings, groups of Christians in various educational institutions, and through being linked with para-church organizations or mission agencies. More and more mission boards are establishing programs to assist in this area. Often they have prayer bulletins or booklets which they send to their constituents. This can help greatly with intercession that is needed for those going abroad to foreign universities. As Fraser, who was a missionary in Lisuland, stated, he was only on the front lines as one gathering intelligence and it was the prayer warriors at home who were actually fighting and winning the battles against the powers of darkness.[8]

The Inter-Varsity Christian Fellowship has a fine program, Student Training in Missions. For this they not only give good orientation, but also encourage those who are preparing to go abroad to get to know international students from their assigned country and correspond ahead of time with Christians in that land, if at all possible. This project is just for a summer. And students work right along with missionaries and national Christian leaders in communicating the gospel across cultural barriers. They help by teaching vacation Bible school in national churches, working in camps, and in teaching English to university students. Inter-Varsity Christian Fellowship also provides a unique and helpful program designed to assist Christian students going abroad. They can be put in touch with national Inter-Varsity groups in various countries which are associated with the International Fellowship of Evangelical Students.

Campus Crusade for Christ has a very fine orientation program under their Agape Movement. Dr. Larry Poland is in charge. They also are hoping to expand into the area of assisting mature Christian students to go to study in universities around the world.

The Navigators, who have work in many countries, specialize in discipleship. For this area of Christian nurture, they put out excellent materials and encourage effective methods to help Christians grow.

Another fine Christian organization which can help students in many countries is Youth with a Mission. They provide Schools for Evangelism in various countries where practical training is given in the art of leading people to Christ.

For some years, Operation Mobilization has encouraged students to enroll at universities in various countries, especially those which are closed to regular mission work. Along with their study, these young people have also been able to do much with Scripture and Christian literature distribution. They have also been able to welcome, house, and assist other Christian young people who come into these countries on a short visa basis.

Young Life Campaign is also expanding internationally and can be especially effective in assisting with the reaching of high-school-age youth. Youth For Christ International has autonomous associations in over fifty different countries and thus can be helpful for those studying in nations where this work has been established.

Students planning to study abroad can also check regarding denominational and interdenominational mission boards working in various nations. These are listed by countries at the back of *Mission Handbook: North American Protestant Ministries Overseas,* published by World Vision's MARC. These mission agencies can give valuable assistance in the area of orientation and preparation, in arranging possible contacts with missionaries on the field, and in assisting with linguistic and cultural studies. They can also help with introductions to national Christians. These agencies often have short-term mission service opportunities, extending from a summer to a couple of years in duration. This is valuable experience for young people, not to mention the contribution they make to the ministry. Statistics have also shown that 25 percent of the short-termers return to the field as continuing career missionaries.[9] Some mission agencies also have short-term opportunities for young people to teach English in various countries. To do this the Bible is often used as the text, and many have been led to Christ by this means.

There are also many American and Canadian government-sponsored study programs abroad. One can get information on these from the registrar's offices in various universities, from reference materials in libraries, from the International Communication Agency of the State Department, and from the Cultural Affairs Offices of various embassies located in North America. Through student exchange programs, North American young people are already studying in Communist China.[10]

In regard to the tremendous opportunities young people have today to enter universities and educational institutions all around the world, the words of the great missionary Francis Xavier (1506–1552) are more apropos than ever: "Tell the students to give up their small ambitions and come Eastward to preach the Gospel of Christ."[11]

13/INVESTING
YOURSELF FOR CHRIST

The master . . . returned and settled accounts (Matt. 25:19, NIV).

Margaret Nash, in her book *Christians—World Citizens,* states,
"The governments of developing countries, when asked their most
urgent need, say repeatedly: 'Help us develop ourselves'; i.e., send
us those who by their teaching will enable us to provide our own
doctors, engineers, bankers, and teachers."[1] Dr. Howard
Mattsson-Boze, who served as a tentmaker by teaching in Tehran,
echoes this need.

Many are actively seeking places abroad where they can use their
secular skill as a means to Christian witness. Opportunities for
such work overseas seem to be increasing, as developing nations
seek skilled workers to help them achieve economic and social
goals. In many areas there is a shortage of middle level
management, in others they need engineers, almost everywhere
there is a dearth of medical personnel, and teachers are usually in
demand. These openings offer tremendous opportunities for
Christians to be of service by their skills and integrity.[2]

Chua Wee Hian, general secretary of the International
Fellowship of Evangelical Students, also sees tentmaking as a key
opportunity in reaching areas closed to regular missionaries. He
writes:

We have been faced with the problems of "tough fields." Today, however, we are seeing the ploughing up of these difficult lands. With the thirst for technical knowledge, Middle East and North African governments are recruiting skilled personnel to teach and train the young. It is our prayer that Christians will take this opportunity of working in secular fields by supporting themselves as "tentmakers" and at the same time share their faith informally and naturally. For the present this seems to be the most effective way of reaching key Muslims for Christ.[3]

Dr. Walter M. Furbay, chairman of the Department of Business and Economics at King's College, who worked as a self-supporting Christian witness in East Africa, states that tentmakers are needed to assist those nations in the following areas: construction, communications, transportation, flood control, water conservation, irrigation, deep-well digging, improvement of agricultural methods, provision of grain storage facilities, preservation of food, child-care centers, crafts, industries, marketing, and distribution.

TEACHING OPPORTUNITIES

Professor Herbert Kane of Trinity Seminary, who was formerly a missionary in China, believes that teachers have the greatest opportunity to be tentmakers. He writes, "In the Orient and to a lesser degree in Africa, the teaching profession is held in high esteem. The teacher is dealing with young people who are still in the process of intellectual maturation, open to new ideas. The students of today are the leaders of tomorrow. As such they represent the greatest potential."[4] I, too, found this to be true when I was teaching under the Ministry of Education of the government of Afghanistan. Whenever I would enter the classroom, the students would stand. Although I had to be very careful what I said in class, because one of them had been assigned to report to the secret police anything I said that was out of line, nevertheless this afforded an opportunity to get to know these students in a well-thought-of context. Professor Kane also notes that a teacher usually works within a highly structured program in an institution, knows exactly what to do, can go to work immediately, and therefore can have the satisfaction of making a worthwhile contribution.[5]

With English the *lingua franca* of the twentieth century, there is a great hunger around the world to study it. Today many institutions offer good courses in modern and effective ways of teaching English which can be of tremendous assistance. In Afghanistan, the desire to learn English was so great that besides teaching in a government high school, I was asked to take special classes with members of the Ministry of Foreign Affairs for seven years. I was also called on to give English lessons to the Crown Prince in the Royal Palace.

"Teaching English is an area wide open to a foreigner," writes a Christian in the Middle East. "Advertisements appear in the newspapers offering top salaries and benefits to qualified teachers. Such positions require appropriate degrees and experience."[6]

An American Christian in Turkey at first hesitated to become a teacher of English, thinking this would take too much of his time. But now, by teaching eight hours a week, he is able to get a visa. He also is more respected and accepted by the people and has many opportunities to share Christ with them. Another friend wrote about his experience in Spain: "My best opportunities for evangelism were with two of my English students."

Because of the great desire for education around the world, "the vast majority of American Peace Corps volunteers are engaged in teaching,"[7] Dr. William Threlkeld of the Navigators writes, "University employment is an outstanding opportunity. We have a missionary associate in several universities overseas, and they are having a fruitful ministry, as well as making an effective social contribution in the context of their jobs."

LOCATING BUSINESS, INDUSTRIAL, AND PROFESSIONAL POSITIONS

Securing a tentmaking job abroad is very much like getting a position at home. One usually has to apply personally through professional employment agencies, newspaper advertisements, acquaintances, multi-national companies, educational foundations, industries, hospitals, nonprofit philanthropic foundations, or government offices. Those planning on a tentmaking ministry can also research their own professional journals for listings.

Overseas Counseling Service operates a comprehensive computer matching service to assist Christians in securing positions abroad.

Wayne W. Shabaz, who served as a tentmaking businessman in the Middle East, has initiated a personnel service to assist qualified Christians secure positions abroad. Shabaz assists with orientation through the services of Missionary Internship.

Ruth Siemens also has a service named Global Opportunities that helps prospective tentmakers. Having had a great deal of experience abroad as a tentmaker and a planter of Christian student fellowships, she can advise from her practical background regarding the securing of and preparing for positions abroad.

Personnel offices of certain mission boards can also help Christians locate positions in various countries.[8] For example, the Sudan Interior Mission is helping recruit teachers for the Nigerian government, which is including the teaching of the Bible in its public schools.

The United Nations services in developing nations include the following: city planning, refugee work, emergency help to children, medical assistance under the World Health Organization, the Food and Agricultural Organization, educational, scientific, and cultural programs under UNESCO, reconstruction, development and financing under the World Bank, the International Labor Organization, the Universal Postal Union, the International Telecommunication Union, the World Meteorological Organization, the International Civil Aviation Organization, the International Atomic Energy Agency, the Disarmament Commission, The Inter-Government Maritime Consultation, the General Agreement on Tariffs and Trade, as well as personnel for international peace forces. Professional needs for the various divisions of the United Nations can be secured from the secretary general's office.

Positions sponsored by the U.S. government to assist Third World countries can be located through the Agency for International Development (USAID). Positions with the Peace Corps and Vista can also be secured through ACTION. There are also other government-supported programs, such as the Fulbright-Hayes Scholarships, which sponsor university lecturing positions and research abroad.

There are over 400 nonprofit organizations in development assistance abroad which have personnel needs. The Christian Service Corps helps recruit and train skilled lay persons between the ages of eighteen and seventy, who usually serve two-year assignments. This has been called the Christian counterpart of the

Peace Corps. Inter Link is another association which seeks to assist Christian business and professional people in developing resources abroad for the benefit of others.

It is usually better to secure a position abroad through an office in one's home country, whether it be the U.S., Canada, or a European nation. Travel to and from the country is then provided, and backing can be secured from the office where the hiring was done.

Some employers seek to include a conflict-of-interest clause in the contract. And even though religious matters are usually avoided in the terminology, this is an attempt to seek to restrict such freedoms. In spite of the difficulties involved, investing yourself for the Lord abroad can have great benefits in this life and throughout eternity.

MEDICAL OPPORTUNITIES

Some Christian doctors, dentists, and nurses are volunteering for short periods overseas. Most of them pay their own way. A heart specialist, Dr. Richard M. May, who served a short time in Africa, states, "Before I went to Congo, I had more or less ignored the cause of missions. But after three months of exposure to the overwhelming needs of the Congolese and to what the church is doing to meet them, I am convinced missions is the most effective and important force for good in the world today."[9] Dr. William C. Ostrom, a graduate of Harvard Medical School with a specialty in ophthalmology, as a young man signed a Student Volunteer card, stating that he planned to become a foreign missionary. Even though he was kept from this, after retirement he paid his way to Afghanistan, donated his medical equipment to the National Organization for Ophthalmic Rehabilitation, and served on a voluntary basis.

The Christian Medical Society and MAP International, as well as certain mission boards, have volunteer programs to recruit doctors, nurses, and dentists who can assist with such needs around the world. These medical people usually pay their own way and serve on a short-term basis. More and more Christian groups of physicians and dentists are staggering their work so that each member of their team can take a turn serving on a mission field on a voluntary basis.

CHRISTIAN TOURISTS

Christians are now able to travel to all parts of the world as tourists and have an unprecedented opportunity to witness along the way. One who visited the Holy Land was able to lead his Muslim guide to Christ and introduce him to Arab Christians for follow-up and fellowship. A leaflet titled "Unofficial Missionaries" has the following tips for Christian tourists:

Be courteous and kind to each person you meet. Respect local customs. Never ridicule their views. Positive expression in word and action as to the meaning of Christ for your life is always the best witness. Avoid referring to people of a nation as natives. Speak of a person by his nationality: a Brazilian, a Japanese, an Austrian, or a national. Don't brag. Be gracious enough to admit that you always have something to learn and don't view differences as inferiorities. Don't be a complainer. The whining tourist is a familiar American export. He does more damage than the Japanese beetle. Dress simply in a manner appropriate for the locality and occasion. As your travels take you around the world, remember that you are communicating the love of Christ to those whose paths cross yours.[10]

CHRISTIAN RETIREES

"There are retired persons who still have five or ten good years ahead of them and want to serve the Lord in the mission field," says Professor Herbert Kane. "Their number is growing with every passing year. Most of them have a pension which renders them financially independent. These older missionaries make wonderful hosts and hostesses in mission homes or house parents in schools for missionaries' children. Others with experience in bookkeeping, accounting, typing, and filing are able to fill vacant posts in mission offices at home or abroad, thus setting missionaries free for more direct forms of service."[11]

Harry Meahl completed his service with the General Electric Company in 1963. He had several inventions he had patented. Instead of going into retirement, he and his wife, Anna, came to Afghanistan. She was hired to teach fifth grade in the Christian school, Ahlman Academy. He came as her dependent. But when the University of Kabul found out about his training and experience, he was asked to set up their electrical engineering laboratory. After his wife completed her teaching contract, they both served as volunteer workers in the Community Christian Church there. They started Bible studies, assisted with prayer breakfasts, called on the sick, met visitors at the airport, entertained guests in their home, helped with Sunday school, directed daily vacation Bible schools, served on church committees, ministered to hippies and world travelers, carried on an in-depth prayer ministry, and led many to Christ. They had nine fruitful and eventful years on the field before Anna died of cancer. Harry had come to love the people, the country, and the work so much that he stayed on alone for four more years. In this way they invested their retirement for Christ.

14/THE CRUCIAL POSITION OF MISSION BOARDS IN TENTMAKING

The Holy Ghost said, "Separate me Barnabas and Saul for the work whereunto I have called them" (Acts 13:2).

"The mission society is the only kind of organization which 2,000 years of Christian experience assures us is able effectively to go beyond normal mono-cultural evangelism and reach cross-culturally to the vast proportion of those who do not yet know Jesus Christ as Lord and Savior," writes Dr. Ralph Winter of the U.S. Center for World Mission.[1] He points out that five-sixths of the non-Christians in the world today are behind cultural barriers, which means that they can be reached only by bridging these. He therefore concludes that mission agencies are essential if the almost three billion unreached people are to be evangelized. He goes on to state:

The great bulk of people on this planet are concentrated in Africa and Asia; the three largest blocks of mankind—the Chinese, the Hindus, and Muslims have only tiny Christian communities, if any at all, related to them. Only a very small proportion of the non-Christians are within normal evangelistic striking range of existing Christians. The only effective answer to the major part of this need can come from specialized cross-cultural organizations of the type represented by a standard mission society, either local or foreign.[2]

Thus, according to the evidence of history, if tentmakers are to be effective in reaching the unreached cross-culturally for Christ, they too must be associated with some sort of mission agency. The Holy Spirit set up a similar structure through the church in Antioch when he called Barnabas and Saul to be sent out on their first missionary journey.

As tentmakers in Afghanistan, the Lord led us to establish a united evangelical mission. This was made up of workers from various agencies. In 1973 there were 135 in this fellowship from thirteen different nations and representing over twenty organizations. These workers were assigned from agencies abroad to the International Afghan Mission.

Considering the largely untapped reservoir of potential evangelistic opportunities with tentmakers, Dr. Willian Danker has written, "The church of the twentieth century on the whole has failed signally to train most Christian businessmen going overseas for personal missionary vocation."[3] Andrew Dymond of the Bible and Medical Missionary Fellowship links this failure with missionary agencies when he writes, "Many tentmakers could be far more effective if they had received more informed advice from experienced missions."[4] Could this be the reason why so many tentmaking schemes fail?

John Kyle, the missionary secretary of the Inter-Varsity Christian Fellowship, writes, "I have noted while working in the Philippines that most of the lay people I knew overseas who made lasting contributions eventually came into fellowship there with the missionaries or Christian workers. Some of us just must be under authority to function correctly. Here is where there is a need for assistance." Thus, unless tentmakers are helped by mission agencies, their work will probably simply be "shadow boxing," as the Apostle Paul puts it (1 Cor. 9:26,TLB).

"The position of the lay worker overseas must be the business of all missionary societies and all churches," writes Robert Kurtz. He goes on to state that orientation for these should not only be provided in the home country, but also on the field. "As soon as lay-workers go overseas, they must be put in touch with the church and mission nearest to their place of work."[5] Stating that the lay worker is becoming a definite type of the missionary of tomorrow, he encourages a close relationship and cooperation between tentmakers and mission societies.[6]

"The missionary in Bangladesh is engaged in Christian service, but so is the Christian oil company executive in Venezuela," states Phillip Butler, founder and president of Intercristo. Professor Kane also exposes the fallacy of this dichotomy when he states, "There should be no rivalry between the two kinds of missionary. Both represent the same Lord; both serve the same cause; both seek to extend the same kingdom."[7]

Dr. Howard Mattsson-Boze explains that this lack of cooperation often comes from tentmakers themselves. "Evangelical Christianity has imbedded in it a strong streak of individualism, and many young men and women set out single-handedly to evangelize the world. This is a desirable goal, but it tends to zeal without knowledge, resulting in either frustration and discouragement or in agonizing reappraisal."[8] Dr. Stanley E. Anderson, who taught four years at Pahlavi University in Shiraz, Iran, bears this out from his experience as he writes:

Were we to go to Iran again, we would try to be affiliated with a U.S.-based organization, be it college, university, industry, or government agency. We would also affiliate with a regular mission board in the country as a field partner. Such could provide one with a fellowship of experienced missionaries already in the country as well as the machinery and benefits of a regular mission board. There is something to be said for the added motivation of accountability to some group in spite of the fact that one is earning one's own support. The Apostle Paul provides a good model for us.[9]

Dr. Mattsson-Boze says:

Association with veteran missionaries who are open to new ideas but who also can guide newcomers and help them to avoid serious blunders is a valuable experience. Coping with landlords, traffic, simple purchases, men-women contacts, and the myriad little frustrations of living in a different society is greatly eased when one has continuing friendships with those who have made adjustments and understand how to ease that transition. Insofar as Christians can learn about the culture through contact with missionaries who understand the problems, they will see the importance of learning the language and the cultural sensitivities. The mission organization should gladly accept the self-supporting missionary and recognize his potential contribution, whereas the self-supporting missionary should equally recognize the values of the more institutionalized, ongoing missionary work. Both have their place. Such mutual recognition could lead to creative cooperation between the two complementary forces: perhaps "associate" status for the self-supporting missionary, enabling him to share in the fellowship and mutual support of the mission while yet leaving him free to pursue what he regards as his own goals. Some of these persons do not have large incomes and therefore need additional financial support in order to permit them to carry on their tasks effectively. They may have large educational expenses for their children, travel costs, and may need more money than a national because of their accustomed way of living. They may also need financial support for a time while they are learning the language. Almost all mission boards recognize the need for a periodic return to the home country for rest, communication with churches and other supporters, and for further training. The financial arrangements for such furloughs are built into the mission structure. But a self-supporting missionary usually has no such provision. If he wants to return home, it is usually at his own expense, and jobs are often unavailable, especially in areas such as teaching.[10]

WHAT MISSION AGENCIES ARE DOING

The *Mission Handbook,* published by World Vision's MARC, states that eighty-four mission agencies reported having persons related to them who are serving in a lay or self-support type of ministry. To find out what was being done I wrote letters to 200 boards requesting information. Most of those who answered stated that they were helping and being helped by tentmakers only on an informal basis, even though they realized they should be doing more. On the other hand, the findings revealed agencies which have seized this unprecedented opportunity and are developing programs of mutual ministry through effective association with tentmakers. Of the mission societies polled, some are *modalities* which represent a whole church or denomination, while others are *sodalities* which have interdenominational constituencies or are backed by special interests within a church. A few of these will be selected to illustrate programs they have. The following in no way is an exhaustive list of the eighty-four agencies which the *Mission Handbook* mentions as having ministries with tentmakers. The ensuing is an initial sampling of what is being done, as culled from the answers returned by various missions. They will be considered alphabetically.

The American Baptist Churches International Ministries has a program whereby local churches are encouraged to recognize persons in secular professions who are about to go overseas as "Ambassadors for Christ." This mission also welcomes volunteers who will pay their own way and will assist in needed areas around the world.

The Bible and Medical Missionary Fellowship has done much to pioneer an effective relationship between tentmakers and their mission. These are called International Service Associates. Though they are financially self-supporting, they subscribe to the basis of faith of the mission and enter into bonds of prayer fellowship and cooperation, being invited to participate in regional conferences and other fellowship meetings. Dr. Raymond Windsor, the general director of BMMF, has written, "Self-supporting Christian witness may outstrip traditional missionary witness in the future. I am disappointed at the slow growth. This may well be because we have not sent tentmakers for deputation ministry in churches and amongst university student groups or people in professions. Most missionaries are inspired to offer for service mainly as a result of face-to-face contact with missionary deputationists. This could be a reason for the slow increase in self-supporting witness."

The Reverend William W. Kerr of the Christian and Missionary Alliance writes, "Without lay people involved in world evangelism, the task will never be completed. Our mission—the C. & M.A.—is presently developing a program designed for all such countries where missionaries cannot go, whereby through seminars, theological education by extension, or night school lay people going abroad in such capacities can get some basic but thorough Bible study, something of the history of the place they are going and studies in cultural patterns. Missions should lead the way in alerting the church of the need for lay people getting involved in Christian witness."

Dr. John Keith of the Canadian Baptist Overseas Mission Board writes of the way they have been able to send letters of recommendation along with Christian lay people who are going into areas where they have mission work. This is very much like the church in Ephesus giving Apollos a letter when he went to Greece (Acts 18:27). Dr. Keith writes, "Laymen are not readily accepted and integrated into the existing group unless they have direct ties with the founding body, and even then unless those ties are somehow or other formalized through correspondence or a recommendation."

The Rev. Edward Van Baak of the Christian Reformed World Missions, who also served as a pastor in Afghanistan, tells of plans to send tentmakers a regularly published letter which will include information helpful to them.

Rufus Jones of the Conservative Baptist Home Mission Society writes, "I am firmly convinced that the way to evangelize the world today is through those who are serving in secular professions in foreign countries. However for them to be effective cross-cultural witnesses, they must not only be familiar with the culture but also have a deep appreciation for that which is good within it. In addition, they must have a love for people and recognize that they were created in the image and likeness of God and that Jesus Christ died for them as well as for us. Above everything else, they must put the kingdom of God and his righteousness first, even above advancing their personal careers or making a profit for the corporations they serve. The Christian ethic must be demonstrated in every decision they make, in every action they take, and in all their relationships to the people with whom they come in contact while in the country."

George Patterson of the same mission, working in Honduras, writes about tentmakers, "We have had considerable experience in this type of coordination between these people and the mission work. Sometimes the results are very positive; often they are very negative. The greatest problem has been that they rarely make an effort to adapt enough to the culture. They do not have enough communication with the people to allow the Spirit of God to cultivate that love which could enable them to attend their churches, sympathize with their needs, and identify with their work. We have also been greatly assisted by Christian businessmen who have visited briefly and helped us reorganize the administrative part of our operations. They help us think through our projections for the future, organizational plans, and more efficient ways to keep books, etc. They also help us find where we can buy supplies and they furnish valuable contacts. Often we are so busy thinking how we can persuade them to give money for our work that we forget that the Lord probably sent them here for us to give them a brief ministry and to enable them to broaden their own horizons and vision. These persons have also helped us write texts for our Extension Bible Institute and for our social work program. A nurse helped write a book on first aid for semiliterates, a dentist helped with one on dental hygiene, a farmer a booklet on raising vegetables, a public health official a publication on nutrition, a student in the humanities a manual on organizing a cooperative, a seamstress a pamphlet on how to sew, and a musician one on church music."

Eugene Bertermann of the Far East Broadcasting Company writes, "Many serving overseas in secular professions who are earnest Christians relate very closely to our broadcasting activities. Our studios in Tokyo maintain a good relationship with the secular community and draw on their ability. This enables them to be more effective witnesses with their professional and political peers and to have a more meaningful relationship with national Christians and indigenous churches. Our experience has been that they are not only financially self-supporting but give substantially to mission work."

The Reverend W. H. Paget, home director of the International Christian Fellowship, writes about the field partnership scheme. "We do have such a plan and feel that it should meet a very real need, but as of this date we have had no response of any kind from anyone! I think that we all need to put this plan before Christian businessmen much more than we have. We need to think how best to reach the potential supply of such tentmakers."

Bill Tarter, president of International Missions, writes, "Professional people assigned overseas have been a tremendous help to us. Now that I think about it I am ashamed that the help has been so one-sided. Doubtless, we should have been prepared to do more for them."

Laura Raab of the Language Institute for Evangelism writes, "For about three years we had a girl work with us who was in Tokyo as a self-supporting witness. She came and taught English two nights a week at our student centers as a volunteer. She enjoyed the fellowship and training, and our ministry there gave her an outlet for the presentation of Christ."

Vernon Wiebe, general secretary of the Mennonite Brethren Missions/Services, mentions that they have a policy to assist those who want to share the Christian faith through their vocation by counseling with them, offering guidance in placement, and preparing them with prayer support and encouragement.

The Navigators have initiated a program for missionary Associates. Dr. William Threlkeld, director of this work writes, "We are excited to see what God is doing in the area of self-supporting missionaries in the world. Our two key requirements are that: 1) an individual be an experienced disciple maker, and 2) an individual have a profession or skill which is marketable overseas in order to be self-supporting. This is a pioneering thrust with us and we are trusting God to show us a step at a time how to develop it. Our experience to date indicates that this is an effective way for individuals to minister for Christ." The Navigator policy paper on this program further states, "The concept calls for qualified disciplemakers who are also trained and experienced professionals, both male and female, to secure positions overseas where they can both work and minister in another country, as team members with other missionary Associates and with Navigator staff. The ideal situation would call for several Associates to work and minister in the same general location. They could take full advantage of the Ecclesiastes 4:9, 10 principle, 'Two are better than one; because they have a good reward for their labor. For if they fall, the one will lift up his fellow: but woe to him who is alone when he falleth; for he hath not another to help him up.' In addition, the locations selected would be close to Navigator staff people. This would allow for consistent overseeing by Navigator staff and would ensure that the Associates would not be alone spiritually or otherwise. In addition, the Associates could relate to local Christian churches and be an integral part of the Christian community overseas. This type of relationship would provide a more effective work and ministry environment and would allow nationals to see a disciple making ministry demonstrated. The job overseas would be for four primary reasons: 1) to earn a living (be self-supporting); 2) to make a social contribution to the people of the country involved; 3) to serve as a base of contact for making disciples; 4) to relate to Christian churches and communities overseas. While Navigators cannot obtain jobs for Associates, we could give guidance and suggestions as to the best opportunities."

William Bell, deputy general director of the North Africa Mission, writes from France, "We have been directly involved in this type of program for about ten years and anticipate that it will be a major part of our total ministry for the foreseeable future. We believe in this approach to the extent that we have created a category of membership which we call Special Service Workers.

Such people are full members of the mission. Out of a total missionary force of about 100, twelve of our people are so involved. All of those had had some general missionary experience before gaining employment, so they were prepared in language training and cultural orientation. Our basic premise is that we are looking for people who have a strong commitment to serve the Lord and who are prepared to use whatever training and experience they have had in order to find places of service. In their system of personal priorities, their commitment to the spiritual ministry will take precedence over the desire to exercise their profession. They will be prepared to give significant time (two-four years) for necessary language and cultural training, even if this means setting aside their profession for a time. We believe that membership in a Mission such as ours offers significant benefits to such people: continuing fellowship and spiritual guidance; administrative help both at home and overseas; a greater possibility of being part of a continuing ministry; the opportunity of moving into another ministry for a time whenever a specific job runs out. We make a guarantee to Special Service Workers to put them on our missionary support list whenever a specific job comes to an end. Primarily for this reason, we encourage them to get personal prayer and financial support the same way as our other missionaries do.

"We have had several experiences where this principle was put into effect. For example, one missionary doctor was expelled from Morocco, where he had had a private practice for several years. He and his family received regular missionary support for about eighteen months before he found another position in a government hospital in Tunisia. In another case, a woman who had been teaching English in Tunisia took a year off to work on a Master's degree. During that year she received regular missionary support.

"Our International Council accepted a recommendation that we hold a seminar annually for Christian professionals with the emphasis on preparation for cultural adjustment and assistance toward effective witness. Such seminars (for two or three days) will be primarily for people going into North Africa, but we are also interested in including people going to the Middle East. If you know any interested in such a seminar, please encourage them to contact us."

The Rev. Abram Wiebe, who is general director of this same mission, states, "People coming out in such a capacity should properly be linked to an existing society either as associate members or in full standing. They will thereby be properly recruited, integrated into life abroad, their ministry will be promoted, they will receive proper orientation, they will be sustained as any full-time worker, they will have some group to identify with [which] identifies with them, and they will receive pastoral care as anybody else in a mission society. I am not an enthusiast for the loner who goes out and plants the church under his own direction and without any supervision. A tentmaker missionary must recognize that there is risk. Very likely, should he be effective he will be asked to leave in a short number of years."

Brother Andrew of Open Doors comments in answer to a letter, "Frankly the project you write about is long overdue. I will pray especially for God's anointing and the necessary cooperation of many Christians worldwide for this very worthwhile project. Speaking for ourselves, we have much work along the line of Christians in secular business, witnessing in restricted areas." Ed Neteland of the same mission writes, "In several of our bases, we have been using people who are in business and have been engaged in Bible distribution and, in some cases, ministry to the people of the suffering Church, because of their access to them in the normal business activities they have."

From Overseas Crusades, James Montgomery, their Director of Overseas Fields, comments, "At this time, we do not have a program that relates to self-supporting witness. If there is an equal percentage of evangelicals among the four million North Americans overseas as there are in the United States—20 percent —that means that there must be somewhere around 800,000 in this category. What a fantastic force for missions and evangelism if this should be mobilized! We certainly will be interested in your book. It could be that this will even provide the information and the incentive for us to become actively involved with these kinds of people."

Another agency that has a program with tentmakers abroad is the Overseas Missionary Fellowship. Dennis Lane, their director in Singapore, writes, "If Christians in self-supporting, secular ministry overseas wish to be associated with a missionary society, it is in fact better for them to be full members rather than to have an unofficial link. We have a number of people who come within this category. One of them is a lecturer in genetics in Kuala Lumpur University, carrying a full program. The Government is aware that she is one of our members, and she prefers it that way.

It means that the entire facilities of the Fellowship are open to her. Another member and his wife, both of whom are qualified geophysicists, are teaching in Indonesia. They have valued being right in with us rather than being on the fringes. In a similar way we have had people teaching zoology part-time in Bangkok, surgery in Chiengmai University in North Thailand, and one teaching pharmacy in another university. This man, during his time in the pharmacy work, was able to start what has now become the Thai Christian Students, the equivalent of Inter-Varsity. The advantage of their being full members of the Fellowship has meant that we could negotiate with the university to ensure that they had adequate language study to communicate with the students before taking their appointment. During that time the Fellowship could support them. We have also been able to provide medical care. On some occasions we have been able to arrange a part-time ministry in the profession, thus giving them more time for their Christian witness. Certainly in Asia the lecturing load that is placed on the university staff is extremely heavy. By being able to provide the extra financial support that enables a person to be part-time in teaching, we can safeguard against this overloading. If people want to have a full link and to share with us, their salary goes into our common fund as members in the general income of the Fellowship. But even though there may be no official link, we do like to have a ministry to such people, and welcome their fellowship."

Executive Director Carmen W. Lynn of the Overseas Missions Department of the Pentecostal Assemblies of Canada writes, "We have had a few of our church members go overseas with industry or government agencies. We have publicized this under the general heading of 'Vocational Missionaries.' These self-supporting lay people have been very closely integrated with the missionary fellowship activities. They actually have been considered a part of our work force in most cases. We give extensive publicity to our Annual School of Missions and open it to lay people who have overseas interests. This is in addition to those persons recruited as missionaries who teach in government-sponsored schools in Kenya with government salaries subsidized by the Overseas Missions Department. These are treated as regular lay missionaries and are expected to take such orientation as we are able to give in Canada and courses for language learning in Kenya."

Another agency in Canada which is actively involved with tentmakers is the Board of World Mission of the Presbyterian

Church in Canada. Earle Roberts, their Secretary for Overseas Operations, writes, "Our Board of World Mission has for a number of years been conscious of the missionary potential available through people in secular employment overseas and has a department known as 'Laymen Abroad.' When a Canadian Presbyterian accepts a job in an overseas country, our Board may, at the request of the individual and using its own discretion, recognize him/her as a missionary. The person might be employed by an overseas nation, university, industry, or the Canadian Government. In considering the recognition of such people as missionaries, we require them to go through the usual candidate procedures for appointment. If accepted, they are designated by a Presbytery and then given the fullest orientation that is possible to work out with their employing body. They are responsible to the Board of World Mission for regular reports on their work and must undertake a reasonable amount of mission education upon completion of each term of service overseas. The Board of World Mission recognizes that this person's missionary calling can be fulfilled through his secular assignment in his normal witness of life work. Our Board relates the person to a church in the country where he serves and looks to that church for pastoral care. . . . The Board normally assumes no financial obligation except for the costs involved in orientation and for such other assignments to which the Board may send the person.

"Through this program we try to get in contact with as many Canadian Presbyterians as possible who are going abroad, either for employment or as tourists. We are having an increasing number of people who are contacting our Board and inquiring about the possibility of volunteer service overseas. Many of these are older people but a few are middle-aged. They offer their services at no cost apart from transportation and accommodation. These people have either private means or have taken early retirement and will live on their pension. Many of these folks are very highly qualified and their skills can better be used by secular agencies than by overseas churches. Our Board is prepared to appoint these folks as special missionaries, when we feel that they are suitable, and second them to an overseas assignment which is most suited to their abilities."

Dr. G. Thompson Brown, director of the Division of International Mission of the Presbyterian Church in the United States, writes, "Recently we have encouraged the appointment of

'Volunteers in Mission.' We just commissioned eighteen of these missionaries. These workers are not paid salaries, as the Mission Board does not assume responsibility for their support other than travel and minimal living allowances in some cases. Many of these are young people who have finished college or technical school and volunteer their services abroad for a year or two. They are assigned to institutions, churches, and schools to whom we are related. We have a growing number of missionaries who may serve on the faculty or staff of secular universities or institutions abroad and whose salaries are paid at least in part by the respective institutions."

The Regions Beyond Missionary Union also has established a Mission Associate category for Christian business people and professionals who are earning their own living overseas and who wish to identify more closely with this agency and share in its ministry. Those who apply are expected to have the same spiritual qualifications as applicants for regular missionary positions.

The Southern Baptist Convention has a special division of its Foreign Mission Board for Laymen Overseas. They estimate that they have nearly 100,000 Southern Baptist church members serving abroad. They are carrying out a full program to minister to these as well as to encourage them to become witnesses for Christ where they serve. This has been included as part of their plan for a total missions thrust for global discipleship by the year 2000. Dr. William Eugene Grubbs, who heads up this department as Consultant on Laymen Overseas, was a missionary in the Philippines. SBC church members serving abroad are alerted to inform Dr. Grubbs' office of their status. The information needed includes the name of the person, the destination, the length of stay, the employer, the names of the family members going along, the ages of the children, and if possible a statement about their spiritual condition. Following this, a packet of material is sent, usually to their pastor, so that it can be delivered personally with an opportunity to discuss the responsibility for mission involvement. This also provides a chance for prayer.

The material is prepared specifically for each person or family and contains: 1) The name, address, and information on an English-language church, if there is one, along with a leaflet entitled "Scattered Abroad," describing the ministries of such congregations overseas. 2) The name and address of the pastor or missionary to be contacted on the field before departure or on arrival is also given. Along with this, two booklets are provided: first, a "Missionary Directory" listing alphabetically all of the Southern Baptist workers abroad with their addresses and type of work; and a second giving the names of their over 2700 missionaries divided into the eighty-four countries and territories around the world where they work. 3) They are also given a booklet entitled "Southern Baptist Laymen on Assignment Abroad" which has suggestions for adjustment to life overseas, and for witness and for service while living there. 4) Enclosed is another pamphlet briefly describing each country where the missionaries are working, entitled, "Know Your Baptist Missions." 5) A further publication, "Unofficial Missionaries," is included, with information helpful for those traveling abroad. 6) Also provided is a suggested dedication service to be held at the end of a regular time of worship in their church. This takes about five minutes and involves a commitment on the part of those going to be faithful in daily Bible reading and prayer, to become part of a congregation as soon as possible upon arrival abroad, to look for ways to be involved in national churches, to seek to support mission work, to try to communicate the gospel across all types of barriers, and to make their home a place where Christ is openly acknowledged as Lord. The pastor and the congregation then pledge to be faithful in prayer and continued interest. 7) Further detailed information is also supplied on special areas of the world to which the tentmakers are going. 8) They are also encouraged to subscribe to the monthly missionary magazine entitled *"The Commission."* Dr. Grubbs further also notifies the pastor of the English-language church or a missionary serving in the area to which the lay person will be going.

The Foreign Mission Board also has a Missionary Associate Program. This enlists lay people who pay their own travel and maintenance abroad, but who assist regular missionary work as physicians, dentists, medical personnel, administrators, teachers, houseparents, agriculturalists, construction foremen, bookstore managers, social workers, and camp directors. They also have a two-year Missionary Journeyman Program for college graduates who are under twenty-six years of age. Even in the U.S., 9,415 of 35,073 Southern Baptist ministers were bi-vocational pastors.

When my wife and I were in Tehran, Iran, in 1973–74 we saw the Southern Baptist Laymen Overseas Program in action. Not only did they have a live English-language congregation which met early Sunday morning in an Iranian Evangelical Church building, but also many of these tentmakers were carrying on an effective witness for Christ among those with whom they worked.

"The Sudan Interior Mission has always appreciated the fellowship and help of Christian expatriates who are living and working in Africa where we are privileged to serve," states Hedley Waldock. "I look back on fellowship with many who were teachers in Government schools, universities, members of the U.S. Embassy, military personnel, employees of airlines and others who were keen Christians, a source of blessing to many. We have a category of mission personnel we call affiliates. An example of this is the current program of assisting the Nigerian Government in finding teachers for its Universal Primary Education program. The Government's plan to introduce universal primary education calls for a great increase in the urgent need of instructors to fill the colleges that train teachers and indirectly the secondary schools of the country. SIM is seeking to assist in finding Christian teachers who look upon this as a great avenue of witness. To those who meet SIM standards we are offering affiliate status. This means that SIM both here and in Nigeria will assist them in preparation and orientation. They will also be eligible to use SIM facilities and their witness and spiritual life outreach will be tied in with the Evangelical Church of West Africa. Moreover, they will be considered a part of the family, and thus there will be opportunity of fellowship both with the Mission and the Church."

The United Church Board for World Ministries (U.C.C.) has an Affiliate category for members who serve overseas as tentmakers. Secondly, they have an Associates program with more than 100 persons a year serving abroad in church-related work on salaries other than those paid by the mission. Screening is done either by the Board or by the hiring organization. They have a third designation called Volunteers who are people who usually pay their own expenses and serve for a limited time. These include teachers, doctors, dentists, and those on sabbatical leaves.

The New York Times ("Missionary Role Under Revision," Aug. 12, 1973) states that there are 50,000 or so Presbyterians living and working overseas. Responding to this opportunity, the Program Agency of the United Presbyterian Church in the U.S.A. has established a category called "Overseas Associates." In 1976, they had over fifty of these serving in eighteen countries. They are assisted by orientation and liaison with the Christian community abroad. Their names are included in the "Mission Yearbook of Prayer." The Program Agency also seeks to help them with services on their return to the United States.

The Rev. Nelson Malkus, executive secretary of World Presbyterian Missions, writes that they have instituted a new category of Field Partners. "We are very very interested in helping such people in any way that we possibly can and we presently have one young lady and three couples under this designation."

The World Evangelization Crusade has also developed a program to accommodate believers who are working in secular positions abroad. It is called Christians in Service Overseas (CSO). Benefits derived from this association are in the area of recruiting, orientation, fellowship, pastoral oversight, and prayer support. "These people experience God's call on their lives, but believe that he will use their profession or skills as the avenue for entering a country and communicating Christ." Will Longenecker, their coordinator in the Middle East, has written, "At the present time we have those who are engineers, professors, doctors, nurses, expatriate pastors, secondary school teachers, carpenters and students in study programs abroad. We require at least one year of Bible training or its equivalent and about 4–6 months of orientation. We feel that a person who desires to go abroad to use his profession as a vehicle and means to present Christ cross-culturally to those with whom he works and to those around him is foolish to think that he will be able to accomplish this unless he has some orientation and unless he has a good grasp of the Word of God. Another great barrier is that of language. Unless we can come to grips with these basic problems, we shall not be able to unleash the power that is wrapped up in so many Christians serving abroad. One of the main burdens of my heart is that here lies a vast resource of spiritual dynamic that is not being tapped."

Professor Herbert Kane describes the advantages a tentmaker has through formal association with a board when he writes, "It is possible nowadays to be a member of a mission with all the rights and privileges pertaining thereto, and at the same time hold a teaching position in a secular college or university."[12]

Phill Butler, the founder of Intercristo, in observing the way more and more mission agencies are becoming involved with tentmakers, has written, "It seems there is a ground swell emerging here at long last!"

15/PREPARATION
AND ORIENTATION

If the iron be blunt, and he do not whet the edge, then must he put to more strength: but wisdom is profitable to direct (Ecc. 10:10).

"Hendrik Kraemer has spoken of laymen as the 'frozen assets' of the church," states professor William Danker in his book *Profit For The Lord.* "There has been much missionary talk about the lay apostolate as the great mission force of the future. Without training, the vast Antarctica of the lay apostolate is not going to be thawed out."[1] As was seen in the last chapter, mission agencies are the bottom line when it comes to effective preparation and orientation. They can cooperate in this with seminaries, Christian colleges, Bible institutes, and other training organizations. Phill Butler of Intercristo says:

One of the most refreshing trends is the large number of architectural, engineering, business administration, and agricultural (to name a few) graduates lining up for Bible programs to equip themselves for genuine Christian service. The self-supporting missionary must have specialized orientation. The international community overseas has its own unique problems and hazards—spiritual landmines abound. We must train these people for cultural sensitivity, linguistic ability, spiritual survival in a hostile environment and methodology in witness.[2]

Professor Herbert Kane also warns, "Those going into this type of service should be better trained than regular missionaries

because of the difficulties of their task." Andrew Dymond, who is
a Field Partner with the Bible and Medical Missionary
Fellowship, writes, "Unless a Christian has some orientation to
adaptation and outreach for Christ across cultural barriers, he will
usually gravitate to those of his own background in the Western
community where English is spoken. The majority of tentmakers
thus find it difficult to fulfill their desire for an effective
cross-cultural ministry."[3]

SPIRITUAL PREPARATION

Our Lord's diagnosis of the witness of many of the religious
leaders of his day was, "You are in error because you do not
know the Scriptures or the power of God" (Matt. 22:29, NIV).
Furthermore the greatest of all tentmakers, the Apostle Paul spent
three years in the Arabian desert to prepare spiritually for his
ministry. Professor Kane comments that

to be effective in their witness [tentmakers] should spend at least a
year in a Bible college or seminary. Today's emphasis in the
homeland on the role of the laity in Christian witness and in
worship is bound to encourage church members to think in similar
terms with regard to overseas service. There are millions of
Americans travelling and residing overseas. [4]

It is the proclamation of the biblical message about Jesus Christ
that God uses to bring people out of spiritual death into eternal
life. If, therefore, tentmakers are to be effective witnesses, they
need to know and trust the Scriptures. In high school, university,
and seminary, I was taught that the Scriptures were full of
contradictions and errors. But in studying them, I found that the
attacks broke down, as the problems presented had answers. I
therefore came to accept the Bible as the inerrant Word of God.
Following this decision I had the joy of leading a friend for the
first time to a saving knowledge of Christ.

My father, who was a missionary in Iran for twenty years,
testified that the courses he had taken in English Bible had helped
him most while he was abroad. A good grasp of the Scriptures
enables one to give reasonable answers to any who ask. With the
world situation being as it is, tentmakers never know when they
may be in a situation where they could be kept from having a

copy of the Scriptures. Watchman Nee, the great Chinese Christian, was imprisoned without a Bible in a cell a little over one meter wide and less than three meters long for twenty years. He had to depend on his vast memory, since for years he had read the New Testament through once a month and the Old Testament through every three months. One of his guards testified how he had come to Christ through the witness of this humble man of God in prison. Ten days before his death on June 1, 1972, he wrote his sister-in-law, "Inward joy surpasses everything."[5]

Dr. William Miller, for many years a missionary in Iran, has said that the reason there are so few converts to Christ in many areas of the world is not so much because of the perversity of the fish as it is because of the paucity of the fishermen. Through the dispersion of tentmakers there are now potential witnesses all over the world. But they need to be taught how to become fishers of men. Learning to lead a person to Christ is essential. Many Christian organizations have good training available in this area.

Not only is it essential to be assured of one's own salvation through faith in Christ, but also it is vital to be filled with the power of the Holy Spirit. I believe one reason God is pouring forth his Spirit in such a wonderful way today is for the purpose of completing Christ's commission of world evangelization.

Even though tentmakers may be self-supporting financially, they cannot be self-supporting spiritually. They need prayer backing from other Christians. The Apostle Paul requested intercession on the part of believers in many of his New Testament letters. Regular missionaries often get prayer support from those who back them financially. But tentmakers need to arrange for it. This is all the more reason why it is important to have an association with a mission agency which can include tentmakers in prayer bulletins along with other missionaries.

EDUCATIONAL PREPARATION

Before leaving for abroad, one needs to read as much as possible about the place of assignment, its history, geography, politics, and economics. Much can also be learned by meeting and talking with people from those countries who are in one's vicinity.

Courses in linguistics are also very helpful. Even though it is usually best to learn the language on the field, training such as is

offered by the Summer Institute of Linguistics can greatly
facilitate a mastery of the tongue. Some have said that with this
training they have been able to learn languages twice as quickly
and twice as well. If one is able to get tapes or records of the
language made by a national speaker, they can be very helpful,
even prior to going to the country. These often provide an
opportunity to repeat what one hears phrase by phrase and thus
help get the sound system and intonation patterns. But check to
make sure it is the dialect needed. An American Army colonel
studied Persian for two years before coming to Afghanistan only
to find he had the Tehran rather than the Kabul dialect, which
proved to be practically useless there. Usually the best way to
learn is first by hearing and speaking, and later by reading and
writing. When one gets to this stage, using a Gospel or the New
Testament in a modern translation of the language along with
English will increase reading ability rapidly, since one avoids
wasting hours looking up words in a dictionary. It is like having
the meaning available on a computer display. Portions of
Scriptures in many languages can be obtained from the American
Bible Society.

Most mission agencies have their own publications and are
happy to recommend reading lists. Other helpful materials can be
secured from the following: 1) The William Carey Library offers
books on missions at reasonable prices. By subscribing to the
Church Growth Bulletin, one automatically becomes a member of
the Global Church Growth Book Club and thereby is entitled to a
40 percent discount on most items. 2) The Evangelical Missions
Information Service provides news bulletins of the Lord's work
around the world, special area studies, and the *Evangelical
Missions Quarterly.* 3) The magazine *Christian Life* also has
helpful articles. 4) *Christianity Today* keeps one well-informed
regarding current mission thinking. 5) The monthly leaflet *The
Church Around the World* provides news items regarding missions.
6) The magazine *Eternity* also has good missionary coverage. 7)
International Review of Mission is published quarterly by the
World Council of Churches and usually represents the viewpoint
of mainline churches. 8) *Missiology* is a scholarly periodical in the
field. 9) Helpful correspondence courses in missions can be
obtained from Moody Bible Institute. 10) *Moody Monthly*
magazine also carries relevant articles on missions. 11) *The World
Vision Magazine* is informative and demonstrates what

evangelicals are doing in social action around the world. 12) The
Missions Advanced Research and Communication Center
produces the helpful *Country Profiles,* which gives a brief
description of the current situation in each nation. These also
carry short bibliographies at the end of each pamphlet.

For further study, missionary biographies dealing with the part
of the world of interest are inspirational and helpful.

CULTURAL PREPARATION

"One of the major problems a multinational corporation faces,"
states Wayne Shabaz, "is the high attrition rate resulting from so
many employees' inability to adapt to new cultures and societies."
These job dropouts usually result from a failure to secure proper
orientation.

Dr. Donald McGavran, a perceptive missiologist, points out
that "as Christianity flows into the many cultures of mankind,
there is no clash with ninety-five percent of their components."[6]
The main part of any culture is its language. And this in itself is
not evil, since the Bible can be translated into it.

Culture shock results from landing in a strange environment. A
study of the behavioral sciences helps one acquire empathy and
face people with humility rather than with an attitude of
superiority. Gaining an understanding of non-Christian religions in
the area will also greatly assist in orientation. It is also important
to learn about manners, customs, and superstitions as well. For
example, there was an American forester in Afghanistan who
found that tamarisk trees grew there very well. He tried to
encourage their planting, but had no cooperation. He asked me to
try to find out the reason. An Afghan friend explained a local
superstition that evil spirits roosted in the branches of this
particular type of tree, and thus the people were afraid of it,
therefore only grew them in cemeteries. On learning this, he was
able to substitute other varieties which were acceptable to the
people.

PRACTICAL PREPARATION

Guide to Moving Overseas by Cathy S. Phelps has helpful practical
suggestions. She and her husband served as tentmakers in several
countries.

In applying for a passport, try to get one with as many pages as possible. Since some visas take up a whole page, those who travel extensively can have them fill up quickly.

The Evangelical Foreign Mission Association can give up-to-date information on the cost of living differential for various overseas locations compared to the rates in Washington, D.C. It is also important to check on the local tax situation in the area. In Afghanistan, we faced a new high income tax which was declared to be three years retroactive.

It is usually best to make arrangements for a trip abroad through a travel agent. Commissions are paid by the airlines and therefore there is no extra charge. Mission agencies can also assist in this area because of their experience. Some of them have their own travel facilities. When we went to Afghanistan, the position there only paid for my transportation. However, through a Christian mission travel agent we were able to secure two tickets for the price of one.

ORIENTATION OPPORTUNITIES

A person serving abroad is bound to encounter many problems and frustrations. Good orientation assists greatly in overcoming these difficulties. It is important to know how to take care of one's health abroad, how to face political problems, and how to deal with personality clashes.

The following are suggested organizations through which tentmakers can secure orientation:

1) Overseas Counseling Service in Seattle offers extensive orientation materials and services. Contact OCS toll-free 800-426-1343 for complete information.

2) Mission boards, both denominational and interdenominational, usually have good programs. These agencies are listed in *Mission Handbook,* published by World Vision's MARC and updated every three years. This volume gives the names and addresses of hundreds of missions, listing them both alphabetically and by the countries they serve.

3) More and more missiological courses are being offered by evangelical seminaries, Christian colleges and universities as well as Bible institutes.

4) The Agape Movement of Campus Crusade for Christ provides orientation courses which self-supporting witnesses can

take. These usually last nine weeks.

5) The Christian Service Corps offers a twelve-week training program and deals with such issues as the biblical basis for missions, personal spiritual growth, evangelism, linguistics, and cultural sensitivity.

6) The Evangelical Foreign Missions Association sponsors sessions on church growth for foreign missionary candidates each year in different parts of the country. Tentmakers would be welcome to take these as well.

7) Another seminar which is helpful, especially for interpersonal relationships, is the Bill Gothard Institute in Basic Youth Conflicts.

8) The Inter-Varsity Christian Fellowship not only has the Urbana triennial Missionary Convention where representatives from many missions around the world have booths, but it also conducts a Missionary Training Camp in Guatemala.

9) Missionary Internship affords excellent seminars for practical preparation. One of these deals with a Pre-Field Orientation. Another is a ten-day Program in Language Acquisition Techniques, and a third course covers Theological Education by Extension, which has become such a vital program around the world. They also have a session entitled Furlough Missionary Program for those who have served abroad and want to have continuing education.

10) The Navigators specialize in Scripture study courses, memorization systems, and discipleship training sessions, and provide orientation with their Missionary Associates Program, geared to tentmakers.

11) Operation Mobilization specializes in training for dissemination of Scriptures and Christian literature distribution. They also encourage students to enroll in universities abroad. Good orientation programs are held with emphasis on practical and spiritual matters.

12) The U.S. Center for World Mission offers training through its Institute of International Studies, concentrating in cross-cultural evangelization with the main focus on reaching the unreached people of the world.

13) Youth with a Mission has practical courses in evangelism and discipleship which are offered in various parts of the world.

The author will be happy to hear of other orientation programs which would benefit tentmakers.

16/LIFE ABROAD

I came to them . . . and I sat where they sat, and remained there astonished . . . (Ezek. 3:15).

The above verse may reflect Ezekiel's culture shock when he came from Jerusalem to those in captivity in Babylon. The Peace Corps, from its experience in many countries, now warns those going abroad of three periods of depression or culture shock. The first occurs when one arrives in the host country. Initial enthusiasm is replaced by depressive realism. The second time of discouragement usually occurs about the third or fourth month after the initial glamor has worn off. And the final period of psychological dejection coincides with reentry into one's own country after serving abroad.[1] Let us look at these stages of adjustment and consequent depression which usually happen both to Christians and non-Christians alike. What are some hints to help cushion culture shock, which affects everybody to a varying degree?

THE INITIAL PLUNGE

Behavioral scientists often speak of ten cultural universals in any society. These are 1) the language, 2) the technology, 3) the economics, 4) the social life, 5) the government and law, 6) the religion, 7) the arts, 8) the scientific knowledge, 9) the matter of health and recreation, and 10) the education. The following are some suggestions for adjusting to these areas upon entering another society.

The Language. Even though a person is in a country for a short
time, phrases such as greetings and farewells can be learned which
will endear one with the local people. A secretary with the
American Embassy in Afghanistan had been there almost two
years and still did not know that the local greeting was "salam."
Mission agencies usually have good language courses and thus can
assist greatly with this.

As soon as one has mastered some of the understanding and
speaking of the language, reading and writing can be learned, as
already mentioned, through the use of the Scriptures in the local
tongue. Parts of the Bible have been translated into languages
which 97 percent of the people of the world understand. Also by
having a national speaker help in studying the Scripture, this can
be an opportunity for the Lord to open that person's heart to the
truth. The young man who helped my wife and me study the
language when we were abroad, through this reading of the New
Testament became a born-again believer.

The Technology. People all over the world develop technological
skills, especially in relation to the necessities of their everyday
lives. The pace of life in most Third World countries, however, is
slower than in the West. There is usually a much more leisurely
attitude toward time, and hurrying is not looked upon as a virtue.
For this reason, a person living in their environment
has to gear down the speed of life to their pace. As Rudyard
Kipling said, "Here lies the man who tried to hurry the East"—
much more can be accomplished with patience and perseverance.
It has been said of some Western technological experts who
go abroad that they blow in, they blow up, and they blow
out.

The Economics. Most expatriate workers abroad get higher wages,
but this is not always true. One couple now teaching in Africa
have a government salary which is just enough for them to live
on, so they cannot save anything. This is a benefit which an
association with a mission agency can give. It can assist with
furloughs and essential financial matters not covered by some
contracts.

In many parts of the world bargaining is considered an indoor
or outdoor sport that one is expected to play if one is to be
culturally accepted. Also, in many places a natural question is to

ask what a person's salary is. This enables them to discover what one's economic status is, which is considered culturally necessary for one to know. A person can usually give a polite answer without divulging the amount of income. It can be stated that one is getting a bit more or less than one would for a similar job at home, or that the salary is very complicated since it is paid in other currencies and includes travel, stipends, bonuses, etc. Or it can be mentioned that the employer wanted this kept confidential. In spite of this, nationals often find out how much people make, especially if they are paid by the local government.

After gauging a person's financial position, nationals will often ask for loans. The policy we followed was never to lend money to anybody. If a person was really in need and we had the means, we would give it as a gift from the Lord. Or again, if they intended to pay a loan back, we would recommend their doing it through a bank. We also would quote a Middle Eastern proverb which states that lending money is like taking scissors and cutting the bonds of friendship.

The tentmaker's work should be of the highest quality. The company or country has made an investment and therefore expects a good return. As the Scripture says, "Whatever your hand finds to do, verily, do it with all your might" (Ecclesiastes 9:10, NASB).

The Social Life. It is important to master customs of common courtesy as rapidly as possible. Sir Kenneth Grubb states, "One meets too many overseas who have left their manners at home."[2] Also, in other cultures family relationships are usually very important. If a person can keep records of how people are related, this can be very helpful.

Associations with the international community are also vital. Among such one can meet people in great need spiritually and otherwise. In attending cocktail parties in Afghanistan my wife and I were never under pressure to take alcoholic beverages, but these occasions gave us opportunities to minister to these friends. When asked what we would like to drink, we would reply, "Something soft, please." They would invariably have fruit juices or soft drinks available.

A Christian needs to decide where his or her ministry will be. One can easily be completely involved with the international community. On the other hand, if nationals are to be reached cross-culturally, a person must specialize in this. It does not mean however that one cannot minister to both groups.

The Government and Law. Coming from abroad, one is a guest in another nation. As such, one should seek to abide by the laws of the land, except where they conflict with God's higher commands. Our Lord laid down this principle when he said, "Render therefore unto Caesar the things which are Caesar's; and unto God the things that are God's" (Matthew 22:21). The Scriptures also remind us to pray for "all that are in authority" (1 Timothy 2:2). Often while waiting to see officials, rather than becoming exasperated by the delay I found these times to be opportunities to pray for the person I was to visit as well as for all in that office. It was then thrilling to see the way God had answered prayer and had prepared hearts when the interview came.

In dealing with officials, it is wise not to put them in a position where they have to say yes or no. Many dread having to sign anything. Usually it is enough simply to inform them of what you would like to do as a matter of respect for their position. You then can write a letter of thanks stating what you shared; the copy you keep in most cases is sufficient evidence of authorization.

If an official letter of request is necessary, a good way to handle it is to draw up a draft, taking it personally to the official. This then enables him to make changes and corrections before the final copy is submitted. In this way a document in fact has been approved even before it is finally signed.

Recently there have been many revelations of bribery by international companies working abroad. Some say that it has to be done in order to fit in with the local culture. But the Apostle Paul refused to do it (Acts 24:26, 27). Also the Scriptures tell us, "A bribe corrupts the heart" (Ecclesiastes 7:7, NASB). Both the giver and the receiver are guilty in God's sight. The Scriptures are clear that it is never right to do wrong. Even though our Lord lived in one of the most corrupt societies in history, he was without sin.

An official in Central Asia took me aside and said that if I would give him a bribe, which he euphemistically called "some candy," he would greatly reduce the tax I was to be charged on a car. Upon refusal, I had to pay the full amount. The Scriptures say, "If you owe taxes, pay taxes" (Romans 13:7, NIV). Some say that it is impossible to live in certain countries without bribing.

This is not true. Besides going against what the Bible teaches, once a person or company starts it word gets around and those with sticky fingers impede matters until they are paid off. The fact that one does *not* bribe can also be a testimony to Christian honesty which is such a need around the world.

Living in an unfamiliar environment will mean that one is bound to commit some kind of *"faux pas."* As Sir Kenneth Grubb has said of tentmakers, "They will make mistakes, but, if they did not, there would be no need for heaven."³ Furthermore, asking for people's forgiveness is such an unusual occurrence in many areas that it makes them pause and wonder why you are different.

The Religion. Understanding the local religion is vital if one is to witness effectively. Not only can this be done through reading, but also by befriending religious leaders who are usually happy to share their beliefs. In this way one is also able to find "redemptive analogies" which can be used to explain Christian truths in terms which are meaningful within the local context.

The Arts. Studying the literature, poetry, folklore, music, drama, and various forms of art enables one to appreciate the local culture. Furthermore these can be used for the glory of God. People all around the world love their own music. As Christian songs are composed in their poetry and are put to their melodies, they strike a receptive chord in their hearts. It also makes them realize that Christianity is not foreign but fits their cultural forms, which makes them feel at home with Christ.

Even though there were no national Christians in Afghanistan until the 1950s, the carpets nevertheless have Nestorian crosses in their patterns. These designs date from the time Christians used to be in that part of Central Asia. This art form can be used as a conversation piece when one is being entertained in an Afghan home. It forms a natural opportunity to explain the meaning of the cross and the fact that many of their ancestors knew about this, as is evidenced by their indigenous art.

The Scientific Knowledge. Getting to know their theories about cosmology and astronomy enables one to explain further wonders of the universe. This then can lead naturally into a discussion of the way "the heavens declare the glory of God; and the firmament sheweth his handiwork" (Psalm 19:1). Learning as much as possible about the history, geology, flora and fauna of the country gives one further opportunities for spiritual analogies which are appreciated.

The Matters of Health and Recreation. Since the physical bodies of believers are temples of the Holy Spirit, God wants his people to care for them properly. With much of the water around the world contaminated, it is wise to drink it in a purified form, such as with coffee or tea or as plain liquid cooled after boiling. Farmers throughout much of the world use human fertilizer. Therefore, vegetables should be well cooked and raw salads should be avoided. Fruit which is washed carefully is usually safe since it does not grow in the ground.

Along with these precautions it is important to have the immunizations that are recommended. In Kabul at one time there were over thirty cases of hepatitis in the American community. The two embassy doctors who were tentmakers had everyone under their jurisdiction injected with gamma globulin. Following this, there was not one case recorded among those who kept up this treatment. These same doctors traced much of the amoebic dysentery to the unwashed hands of those who prepared the meals. They therefore started a food handlers' course. With microscopes, they showed these nationals germs which came from under their own fingernails. Many of these people had previously thought that germs were just a foreign superstition, since they were invisible. Those who took this course were so impressed with what they learned that they would scrub down like doctors before working with food.

In most cultures it is very important to eat with people, since this involves participating in the covenant of salt, or of friendship. They recognize that food and even water contains salt and therefore eating and drinking together is considered very important. Being entertained in the home of a national, one can eat things that are well-cooked and drink liquids that have been boiled. When it comes to salads and other foods which could be harmful, one can explain that as much as he or she would like to eat it, a weak digestive system prevents this. They usually understand this, since they, too, often have health problems.

Many Christians have participated in fishing, sports, or other types of recreation which the nationals enjoy. This enables a person to get to know them well in enjoyable settings. It is also important to plan regular vacations and home leaves. Our Lord told his disciples, "Come with me by yourselves to a quiet place and get some rest" (Mark 6:31, NIV). We all need spiritual, mental, and physical refreshment.

The Education. This is an area in which Christians have greatly helped people all around the world. Instead of insisting on European or American systems, it is best to adapt education to the local situation.

Not only is education needed for the nationals, but also for children in the international community. When my parents were missionaries in northwestern Iran, schooling was not available and therefore they and other missionaries taught us children the Calvert Correspondence School system at home. In Afghanistan tentmakers started Ahlman Academy for their children. This is a Christian institution and teaches the Bible at every grade level. It has not only helped their children scholastically and spiritually, but also has been used to bring others to a saving knowledge of Christ.

It is important, I believe, to keep children with their families and not to send them away to school. The Bible says that if we do not take care of our own families, we are worse than unbelievers (1 Timothy 5:8). I believe the Scriptures teach that God comes first, our family second, and our ministry third. We were able to keep all three of our children with us through high school. Some of the families in Afghanistan who were in outlying areas had their children study through the Extension Division of the University of Nebraska. They offer correspondence courses for grades 9–12.

In spite of some disadvantages to education abroad, children can benefit greatly from travel and from the rich heritage of experiencing various cultures. It is important that they not only learn to understand and speak the local language but also learn how to read and write it. Being young they are able to master it easily and quickly. Later on in their education they may want to specialize in this language or do research in it. If adequate educational facilities are not available, I believe the whole family should move to a place where such can be secured. It also is important for parents to decide whether they want their children to consider themselves nationals of the country where they grow up or of their homeland. If they are kept in a country throughout their formative years, they develop a loyalty which later can create difficulties in adjustment.

By doing things together as a family, whether it be washing dishes or going on trips, teen-age rebellion can be prevented since young people feel an integral part of the family and their sense of loyalty eclipses the desire to rebel.

AFTER THE GLAMOUR HAS WORN OFF

The second type of culture shock which the Peace Corps has observed sets in after one has been on the field three or four months. Many wives abroad, because they have help to do the cooking, the housework, and the shopping, have time hanging heavily on their hands. They often end up alcoholics attending a round of cocktail parties, playing bridge, gossiping, criticizing the local people, and itching to leave. State Department figures indicate that 80 percent of U.S. wives abroad suffer from some sort of psychosomatic problems.[4]

On the other hand, Christian wives find they can spend more time being faithful in prayer, mastering the Bible, organizing coffees and Scripture studies, doing a lot of reading, helping with mission work locally, teaching Sunday school, entertaining in their home, assisting with secretarial work, teaching English, helping with relief projects, ministering to the handicapped, working in local hospitals, and making the home a center for Christian witness.

THE CULTURE SHOCK OF REENTRY

The third type of depression from culture shock comes, according to the experience of the Peace Corps, after one returns to his or her own country. Changes have taken place, both nationally and personally. Adjustment is aided by frequent furloughs. With modern transportation being rapid, home leaves are much more possible than they used to be and frequent furloughs are very helpful in this regard. We brought our children home for three months during the summer every three years. This meant that they did not lose out in their regular schooling. Also, we as a family kept in touch this way with friends and with people who were praying for us. On two occasions we felt that we should stay for a whole year. This enabled our children to get used to education in their own land as well as develop loyalty for their own country.

For a home leave or reentry after a longer period, an association with a mission is very important. The organization then can assist with matters such as getting a position and settling into a new situation. This is where a warm relationship with a sending local church is also important. Many of the tentmakers from Afghanistan found reentry difficult when they returned home. Very little was done to help them since they were unaware of this problem, but thought returning would be second only to heaven. Michael Griffiths, the general director of the Overseas Missionary Fellowship points out that this is not only a problem for tentmakers, but may be even more acute for those who are fully supported and therefore do not have as much opportunity for positions professionally in their own country. He says, "The missionary who returns home in middle age for health or family reasons may have some difficulty in finding satisfactory employment."[5] It is true that God supplies all of our needs according to his riches and glory, but he usually does it through the help of others. Therefore, Christians should be ready to assist brothers and sisters in Christ who return from abroad and need encouragement and help with their reentry and splashdown.

17/ENGLISH-LANGUAGE CHURCHES ABROAD

*Thus saith the Lord God; Although I have cast them far off among
the heathen and although I have scattered them among the
countries, yet will I be to them as a little sanctuary in the countries
where they shall come* (Ezek 11:16).

The dispersion of Christian tentmakers all over the world presents
a great opportunity for evangelical Spirit-filled pastors to minister
in English-language churches. This also affords the chance for
these ministers to be tentmakers themselves, since most of the
congregations are self-supporting.

Such churches have three main purposes. First of all, they
provide fellowship, renewal, and growth for Christian tentmakers
serving abroad. Secondly, they bring a gospel witness to the
swelling crowds of non-Christian internationalists. And thirdly,
they serve as a base for witness to unreached nationals. In
conjunction with the ministries of missionaries, these
congregations can be stepping-stones to cross-cultural witness
which must take place if the world is evangelized.

THE HISTORY OF
ENGLISH-LANGUAGE CHURCHES

In 1701 the Society for the Propagation of the Gospel in Foreign
Parts was founded in Britain by royal charter.[1] Its purpose was
twofold: to minister to the spiritual needs of British settlers abroad
and to evangelize indigenous peoples. This organization became

the means of establishing Anglican churches in North America, in the West Indies, in India, and throughout the British Empire. These English-speaking congregations were the precursors of the mission societies which were sparked by the tentmaker, William Carey. As noted, Henry Martyn went out under the East India Company in 1806 to minister to the English-speaking civil servants of the British government, only to become an effective cross-cultural missionary and translator of the Scriptures.

Even C. T. Studd, one of the "Cambridge Seven" missionary volunteers and founder of the Worldwide Evangelization Crusade, served the Union Church of Ootacamund in South India from 1900 to 1906. He ministered there in English to planters, soldiers, and government officials. His work for the Lord was so effective that word got around that his church was a place to be avoided unless a person meant to get converted.

THE COMMUNITY CHRISTIAN CHURCH OF KABUL

In December of 1952 the Community Christian Church of Kabul was established, by Christian teachers who were tentmakers. The church was organized on an interdenominational basis with an evangelical statement of faith and I was called to be its pastor. All those joining gave testimonies of their conversion and subscribed to the church's confession. Officers were then elected from the membership and thus were all born-again Christians. The number of those attending the services was usually larger than the membership. Individuals in the congregation made their own decisions regarding the time and mode of baptism, and God wrought clear conversions among those of the international community.

After teaching for four years, I found myself doing what the Afghans say you cannot do, namely, holding two watermelons in one hand. I was teaching English for thirty-five hours a week in the government educational system and was also carrying an increasing ministerial responsibility as the international community grew. Thus a petition was presented to the Afghan government by those associated with the United Nations and various embassies requesting permission for me to be a full-time chaplain. A priest assigned to the Italian Embassy ministered to the Catholic community. Since this precedent already existed, the government granted permission for me to be a chaplain to the Protestants in the country.

I then held services in various parts of the country with internationals working in agriculture, teaching positions, construction, and business. Thus in a land the size of Texas, I became a circuit rider, usually traveling by DC-3 airplane.

Since we did not have a church building, funeral services were held in the old British military cemetery. At one of these, hundreds of Afghans came to show their respect for the Canadian Christian who had died of appendicitis while serving there with the United Nations. I suddenly found myself preaching the good news of Christ's death and resurrection in the open air before a large Afghan congregation. Following the service, the Minister of Education for that nation mentioned that this was the most impressive funeral he had ever attended. He said that the Muslim priests he knew did not know what to say on such occasions and he asked me to write out everything I had said so he could share it with them.

Sunday school and confirmation classes as well as daily vacation Bible schools were started for the children and young people in the international community. With the many blind in the country, the Lord also enabled a work to start among them. They were taught Braille in the local language, and with this some went through the first six grades of their educational system. Christian teachers of the blind were recruited from abroad to assist. Furthermore, for those with eye problems who could be helped medically, a project was started with ophthalmologists and nurses coming into the country.

Since the work in Afghanistan was in the nature of a mission church, a board of trustees was set up in the States to assist.[2] This was incorporated as a nonprofit organization which aided Christian projects in Afghanistan, provided part of our support, assisted with our transportation, and helped with our children's education. As the nation began to open to regular missionaries with special training, the trustees of the Kabul Community Christian Church issued an invitation to the ten missions working on the borders of Afghanistan to meet to pray and plan about the possibility of establishing a united evangelical fellowship. All ten missions agreed to this unanimously and therefore the International Afghan Mission was set up in 1966. (The name

International Afghan Mission was selected because the initials refer to our Lord, the Great I AM. In 1977 the name was changed to the International Assistance Mission, which is incorporated in Switzerland.)

With the expatriate community growing, our homes were not large enough to hold all who wanted to meet for worship. Up to this time it had been like New Testament gatherings meeting in homes. But now it was evident that there was need for a larger place in which to worship, if the needs of the international community were to be met.

Since President Eisenhower was coming to Afghanistan on his Asian tour in December of 1959, I wrote his pastor, Dr. Elson, asking him to speak to the Chief Executive about requesting permission for a church building. The new mosque in Washington had just been built for the Muslim diplomats there and, reciprocally, we needed a church in Afghanistan for the Christian diplomats and others there. President Eisenhower very graciously agreed to this, and on his visit to Afghanistan requested permission from the King. The government finally gave authorization for it to be built.

Christians all over the world contributed toward this building. It was completely paid for as it went up and was dedicated to the Lord on Pentecost Sunday, May 17, 1970. In the service of dedication, a hippie girl from New York City accepted Christ as her Savior.

God used the church to start an outreach to thousands of world travelers who flocked to Afghanistan in the sixties and seventies to get drugs and study Eastern religions. This work is now known as the Dilaram Ministry, a branch of Youth with a Mission, and is headed up by Floyd and Sally McClung. Many young people have come to Christ through this ministry. It was thrilling in the new church to have thirty to fifty of the world travelers attending every service.

But with the law of Islam stating that anyone leaving that religion should be killed, persecution started because of Afghans who found Christ. One Sunday after the morning service, soldiers arrived and started knocking down the wall between the main road and the church building, stating that they had been ordered to demolish the edifice. A German Christian businessman went to see the mayor of the capital who had given the order and told him that if they touched that house of God, the Lord would judge their government. Various ambassadors interceded and the destruction was postponed.

In the meantime, the work with the blind was ordered closed, the children were sent home, and the Christian teachers from abroad were given one week to get out of the country. My wife and I were also forced to leave at this time. Even though we still loved the people there, we did what our Lord told us to do and shook the dust off of our shoes at the airport before we left (Luke 9:5).

After we left, the Prime Minister ordered the congregation to give the building to the government for destruction. The church members wrote a letter to the Prime Minister stating that they could not give the building to anyone since it did not belong to them. It had been dedicated to the Lord. And if he took it by force and destroyed it, he would be answerable to God.

In June of 1973 the government sent in bulldozers and began knocking the beautiful building down. The congregation, instead of opposing, offered tea and cookies to the men who were demolishing it. The soldiers had tears in their eyes. They said they knew it was not right to destroy a house of God, but they were under orders and had to obey.

A secret service report had been received by the government that there was an "underground church" in Afghanistan. They did not understand the meaning of this expression and therefore, having leveled the building, they dug twelve feet down below the foundation looking for the underground church.

The very day the destruction of the church and the excavation of the foundation was completed, July 17, 1973, the government responsible was overthrown. It had been a monarchy for 227 years, but then became a republic. The new government, through the brother of the president, apologized for the destruction of the church building, stating that it was against the law of Islam which allows Christians and Jews to worship within an Islamic nation. Secondly, he said it was against international law, since Muslims are allowed to have mosques in Christian countries. And thirdly, it was in violation of the law of Afghan hospitality which shows special courtesy and consideration to guests.

In spite of the loss of the building, the congregation has continued to meet in a large home. The future is as bright as the promise of God—"I will build my church; and the gates of hell shall not prevail against it" (Matthew 16:18).

ENGLISH-LANGUAGE CHURCHES WORLDWIDE

After my wife and I were forced out of Afghanistan in March of 1973, we spent a year in Tehran. There we got to know the international as well as the Persian, Armenian, and Nestorian churches. At that time there were twenty-one English-language congregations meeting in Iran.

Around the world there are over 100 English-language congregations established by the Southern Baptist Foreign Mission Board alone. As Dr. W. Eugene Grubbs writes, "The story of the development of these churches is one of extraordinary lay involvement under dedicated sacrificial pastoral leadership."[3] About 75 percent of these churches are self-supporting.[4] Many of the Christians in these churches tithe their incomes for the Lord, and therefore are able to help support missionary work locally as well as contribute to the denomination at home.

The Southern Baptist folder which is distributed to tourists and others going overseas states, "Of the early Christians it is written, 'They that were scattered abroad went everywhere preaching the word.' Today this same affirmation can be made concerning thousands scattered abroad in business enterprise, government posts, military service or study. Often these displaced persons—separated from home, church and familiar surroundings—are lonely and bewildered. More often than not they are spiritually starved. They need a place of worship and Christian witness."[5]

The Foreign Mission Board of the Southern Baptist Convention also recruits missionaries to pastor in these English-language churches. Many ministers who have retired from their home congregations have gone abroad to serve with an extended missionary vocation by pastoring such churches. Since the medium for preaching and ministering is in English, they do not have to learn the language.

Some pastors have found this to be such a rewarding experience that they have served in several English-language congregations abroad. One minister from the Reformed Church has pastored congregations in Moscow, India, South Africa, Nairobi, Switzerland, and Israel. Some also minister to several groups at different locations. One pastor not only has over 800 in his congregation in the capital of Saudi Arabia, but also flies around the peninsula holding meetings for Christians stationed in various locations.

The Rev. John R. Collins, director of the International Congregations of the National Council of the Churches of Christ, writes that they are now in touch with 103 English-speaking churches around the world.

The Rev. Ronald C. Smeenge, who has pastored churches in Puerto Rico and Haiti, has organized the International Fellowship of Christians, which has published a "Directory of English-speaking Congregations Around the World." Speaking of Americans overseas, he writes, "This community of people is susceptible to the gospel even more than they were back home. There is an increase in their responsiveness because there is an increase in their awareness of need. Because they have had to experience change, they are open to further change. In Japan, one percent of the population is Christian. In Brazil, however, 43 percent of the 700,000 resident Japanese claim some degree of Christianity. New fellowships of Christians are emerging around the world."

Individual denominations and mission agencies also have established and sponsored English-speaking churches abroad. Most of these have been started by missionaries on the field who have been faced with the need. For example, the Christian and Missionary Alliance sponsors four such churches.

Another whole group of English-speaking congregations around the world are those headed up by chaplains in the armed forces. These not only minister to service personnel, but also to civilians. Various organizations are assisting this military ministry, including the Association for Christian Conferences on Teaching and Service (ACCTS), the Campus Crusade military ministry, the Officers Christian Fellowship, and Youth with a Mission.

A minister who had brought students to an Inter-Varsity Missionary Convention and was himself burdened for missions asked me what he might be able to do abroad. I suggested the possibility of serving an English-speaking congregation in another nation. A while later this letter came from him: "I met you at Urbana '73 in the hallway of the Assembly building on the last night. We stopped to talk. I was then a pastor of a small Reformed Church near Albany, New York. You mentioned union churches and challenged me to check them out. I did when I got home. I heard nothing after that until July '75. We were then invited to serve an evangelical union church here in Gamboa, ∽venteen miles from Panama City. After much prayer, battles of the will, etc., we moved here in January '76—and how God is working! We have had opportunities to speak at other union churches and to direct a camp. Several have given their lives to Christ, one family is on the mend, and two young men are on their way into full service. We wanted to let you know. Oh yes, we pray for the crewmen on ships which pass our back door from all over the world! In Christ, Bill Wilbur, Box 44, Gamboa, Canal Zone."

18/WITNESS
WHILE YOU WORK ABROAD

What is my pay? It is the special joy I get from preaching the Good News without expense to anyone. . . . (1 Cor 9:18, TLB).

Since according to the command of Christ world evangelization should be a tentmaker's primary concern, the question arises about the best ways to witness while working abroad.

FRIENDSHIP EVANGELISM

"The man that hath friends must show himself friendly" (Prov. 18:24). William Carey recognized the importance of this as he wrote, "Missionaries . . . must . . . by all lawful means . . . endeavor to cultivate a friendship with them [the nationals]."[1] Dr. Stanley Soltau, speaking from his experience as a veteran missionary in Korea, states:

Spending time with courtesy calls on officials in an effort to win their respect and sympathy may seem an unfruitful occupation, if not a real waste of time. But the far-seeing missionary will recognize his definite obligation to win the confidence and friendship of these officials, not only for the sake of the salvation of their souls, but also for the greater influence their sympathy will exert throughout the whole territory. The example of Paul's courtesy to Felix and Festus as he made his defense before them is one which should be followed. . . . The future usefulness and effectiveness of his work greatly depends on it.[2]

Dr. Cameron Townsend, the founder of the Wycliffe Bible Translators and the Summer Institute of Linguistics, has shown by his success in Christian diplomacy the importance of cultivating friendly relations with officials and all people.[3] Furthermore the Engel Scale bears out the importance of friendship evangelism since it shows that conversion takes place in a process going through proclamation, persuasion, and cultivation on the part of the communicator, resulting in various steps of response on the part of the receiver.[4]

When different ones went to Afghanistan as tentmakers, religious freedom was strictly limited by the strongly Muslim government. We were, however, free to make friends. Hospitality in our home was a means of carrying out real friendship evangelism.

When I was asked to teach English to members of the Ministry of Foreign Affairs, this gave me the chance to befriend diplomats from that country who later were assigned to embassies in many parts of the world. On more than one occasion I was granted a visa to return to Afghanistan by those who had been my former students, when otherwise my wife and I probably would not have been allowed reentry. Also, the fact that I had taught English to the Crown Prince and to his private secretary enabled us to stay in the country as long as we did just before the church building was destroyed.

PRAYER AND EVANGELISM

The Bible reveals, "We wrestle not against flesh and blood, but, against principalities, against powers, against the rulers of the darkness of this world, against spiritual wickedness in high places" (Ephesians 6:12). The Lausanne Covenant reflects this as it states, "We are engaged in constant spiritual warfare with the principalities and powers of evil who are seeking to . . . frustrate . . . world evangelization."[5] In Afghanistan the people have a tradition that when Satan was cast out of heaven, he fell to earth in Kabul, the capital. When the first Christians arrived there, they could feel the power of evil. There were not only satanic attacks from without, but also personality clashes from within the Christian fellowship. These trials produced bitterness in some, but brokenness in others. As David testifies, "The sacrifices of God are a broken spirit: a broken and a contrite heart, O God, thou wilt not despise" (Psalm 51:17).

The secret of victory comes not only from being strong in the Lord through putting on the whole armor of God, but also from wrestling against Satan through "praying always with all prayer and supplication in the Spirit" (Ephesians 6:18). This was the reason the Apostle Paul repeatedly wrote to Christians requesting their prayers. From Afghanistan we sent out a regular monthly prayer letter to home churches and friends which had requests for every day. This went to hundreds of prayer warriors. It was thrilling to see the way God heard and answered. He not only took care of impossible situations, but also made the witness to Christ effective.

Even though religious freedom was restricted, nevertheless we had the liberty to pray. And God gave unexpected opportunities for witness. A young man from the Institute for the Blind came to visit me. He said that even though he was blind, he had noticed the love in the lives of his teachers and wanted me to tell him about God. It was a joy to share the gospel with him.

EVANGELISM UNDER OPPOSITION

Many parts of the world today, especially those under Islamic and Communist governments, restrict religious freedom. This is nothing new. Our Lord lived under one of the most oppressive regimes known in history. And yet in this context he gave the Great Commission to his disciples to take the gospel to every creature. But he explained that in doing this his followers were to be as wise as serpents and as harmless as doves. Christians need to be discerning and discreet in the way they carry out Christ's command to evangelize the world. Their primary duty and loyalty is to God. Therefore, if governments countermand his clear orders, believers must answer with Peter and John, "Judge for yourselves whether it is right in God's sight to obey you rather than God" (Acts 4:19, NIV). Thus even though Christians are to be loyal to human governments in the civil realm, nevertheless when political authorities infringe the Lord's commands, followers of Christ have a prior responsibility and duty to him. The gospel does not change, and therefore Christians "should earnestly contend for the faith which was once delivered unto the saints" (Jude 1:3). Nevertheless *methods* of sharing the gospel do change, and we are to be wise in the way we evangelize, especially in areas where there is opposition.

In Muslim nations conversion is considered a one-way street. A person may become a convert to Islam, but is not allowed to leave that faith. It needs to be pointed out that not even God forces people to believe, and therefore how can a human government or religion presume to have the right to take on this prerogative?

Communist governments regard religion as "the opiate of the people" and thus restrict religious activities in areas where they are in control. Nevertheless, believers in these nations continue to witness, often at the risk of imprisonment and death. And God is blessing and giving them much fruit, as is evidenced by the growth of the suffering churches.

Spiritual conflict can also come from nominal Christians. In Afghanistan the Lord's work was often opposed by officials from the American and British embassies. Here again, in spiritual matters the primary loyalty of Christians is to God rather than to their country.

EVANGELISM IN THE HOME

The Rev. William Sutherland spent many years as a missionary on the border of Afghanistan. At the end of his service, I asked him what he felt had been the most effective part of his ministry. After thinking awhile, he answered that he believed it was the daily devotions they had in their home. He could point to pastors all over Pakistan who at one time had been his household helpers.

In many areas around the world people are desperately in need of employment. Furthermore, by getting others to help in the home, one is free to spend time in studying, teaching, and ministering to those in need. Also, having daily devotions with those who help has proved to be an effective evangelistic opportunity. Scriptures in the local language can be used and in this way they get to know the Word of God, which speaks to their hearts.

We used to meet daily with our help in Afghanistan. I will never forget the church gardener hearing for the first time the story of our Lord's raising of Lazarus from the dead. As he listened to the account of this miracle, tears began running down his cheeks and onto his beard as he said, "What wonderful power Jesus Christ had to be able to bring a man back to life after he had been dead four days!"

Whenever we had guests in our home for meals, we would offer thanks at the table for the food and would pray for the needs of different ones there in the name of Christ. Muslims have a great appreciation for prayer, and they always would listen with reverence and respect. We also found that pausing to pray before driving, even on a short trip, not only resulted in the Lord's protection but also was a telling witness to Afghans and others traveling with us.

EVANGELISM WITH NATIONALS

People in other countries are not usually as reticent to speak about religious matters as those in the West. They love to ask questions about what one believes. This gives a natural opportunity not only to share one's faith, but also to find out what they believe.

When nationals come to Christ, it is important for them to be joined in fellowship with other believers. They also need to worship in their own language, using their own music so that they feel at home in Christianity. Right from the beginning they should be encouraged to take leadership in their own fellowship. They should be the ones to lead in worship, administer baptism, and direct in the Lord's Supper. The local believers should become self-governing, self-supporting, and self-propagating as soon as possible.

In order to carry out Christ's Commission to teach everything he has commanded, it is important to impart an evangelistic and a missionary vision. Believers should be taught the way to lead another person to Christ. Furthermore, they should be given an appreciation of God's work around the world so that they can participate in reaching the unreached.

EVANGELISM WITH INTERNATIONALS

The international community also affords a great opportunity for witness. It was a joy in Afghanistan to see nominal Christians come to a saving knowledge of Christ. These do not need to be reached cross-culturally. Many of them are hungry for real friendship and love. Along with informal coffees and home Bible studies, good literature can have a great impact. Some in Afghanistan came to Christ in their own homes while reading Christian books. Displays of good literature at the church had an effective ministry. Many internationals had not brought their Bibles with them, and therefore they were happy to have the opportunity of securing Scriptures.

TRAINING IN EVANGELISM

Some tentmakers have been able to take Christian correspondence courses on the field or become involved in theological education by extension in the area where they are working. For example, a Christian engineer in Nigeria was able to take a course in homiletics. After two years of study he was accredited as a local preacher.[6] Since theological education by extension is training for lay Christians, this type of in-service preparation fits in naturally with tentmaking ministries.

Many parachurch organizations are now international. For this reason tentmakers can receive assistance on the field from agencies with work abroad. Campus Crusade now has evangelistic helps translated into various languages. The Gideons not only supply Scriptures for hotels and schools around the world, but also are interested in establishing more camps staffed by Christian laymen in various nations. They now have work in over 100 countries, and the majority of their income in North America has gone for their ministries abroad. The Child Evangelism Fellowship has work in sixty-six countries. They have excellent seminars on ways to conduct childrens' meetings, on the use of attractive materials for boys and girls, and on methods of personal evangelism.

The Scripture says that we should be ready to give an answer to anyone who asks us a reason for the hope that is in us (1 Peter 3:15). Dr. Howard Mattsson-Boze tells of an Iranian student who asked him in class, "Did you come here to convert us to Christianity?" The answer he gave was, "Yes. My purpose here is the same as it was in my teaching in the United States."[7]

19/THIRD WORLD TENTMAKERS

When Priscilla and Aquila heard him [Apollos], they invited him to their home and explained to him the way of God more adequately (Acts 18:26, NIV).

A thrilling development on the Christian scene today is to see the way Third World churches are catching a missionary vision. For example, the Grace Gospel Church in Manila, organized in 1956, now supports forty-seven missionaries in eight Asian countries.[1] But also there are more and more self-supporting missionaries going from Third World countries to other nations. This follows in the biblical pattern of Priscilla and Aquila, who came to Christ in Corinth but became tentmakers in Ephesus.

A Muslim Syrian soldier who came to the Lord as he read the Bible while stationed on the Golan Heights states this about Third World self-supporting witnesses: "I believe if the national church is really to burst into growth, it will come as the national Christians launch out into tentmaking ministries. How much greater an opportunity an Egyptian has by serving the Lord in Algeria or Bangladesh or any country where Arabic is spoken or respected. There are truly no closed doors to the nationals of North Africa or the Middle East." He further notes the importance of preparation for such self-supporting missionaries as he states, "Many young men and women in Egypt and Sudan are willing to serve the Lord in other countries, but are in need of training in Muslim evangelism. God is obviously working in a new way today. I believe our most urgent task is to train and mobilize the nationals of each country, so in the event of a completely closed door for Westerners, the churches will be self-reliant."

A Christian from the Middle East writes, "The Baha'i sect in Iran has spread all over the country very remarkably because of the tentmaking ministries of the followers of that religion. It is time for the local Christians in Muslim countries to make the best use of tentmaking ministries."

The Lausanne Covenant reflects this development among Third World Christians as it states, "We rejoice that a new missionary era has dawned. . . . God is raising up from the younger churches a great new resource for world evangelization." This document continues by stating, "Thus . . . the universal character of Christ's Church will be more clearly exhibited. . . . Missionaries should flow ever more freely from and to all six continents in a spirit of humble service.[2]

THIRD WORLD TENTMAKERS IN AFGHANISTAN

In Kabul there have consistently been a fine group of Third World tentmakers. One of them, Dr. Kintson Keh, a Chinese Christian agriculturalist working with the United Nations, had a great witness in the country. As an elder in the church, he headed up various projects designed to show to people the love of Christ in action. He introduced rainbow trout into the streams and lakes of that land as well as bringing Long Island ducklings to that nation. Not only was he a witness for Christ among the local people, but he was also able to lead other Chinese friends there to a saving knowledge of his Lord.

Caesar Mileton was a Christian tentmaker from the Philippines. He served in the southern part of Afghanistan with an American construction company which built dams and canals. One day while he was driving on the job he saw that an Afghan man had slipped and fallen into one of the giant canals and was drowning. He threw him a rope, but the man could not grab it, so he tied the other end to his truck and dived in to save him. He did not realize that under the surface of the water there were concrete pilings. He struck one of these with his head and did not come up. The Afghan man was able to get a hold of the rope and get out, but Caesar had given his life to save this unknown friend.

Hundreds of Afghans came to the funeral, where the message centered on another who had given his life to save those who were dying. The text was, "Greater love has no man than this, that a man lay down his life for his friends" (John 15:13). This tentmaker had come from an evangelical church in the Philippines. He lived and died in that unevangelized country as a good witness of Jesus Christ.

THIRD WORLD TENTMAKERS FROM KOREA

The University Bible Fellowship in Seoul is a mission agency which provides a model of success in the area of self-supporting witness. It was started by the Rev. Chang Woo Lee as a small indigenous student movement in Korea in 1960. Since then, it has grown rapidly, both in Korea and in other nations. By 1976 they had sent 157 tentmaking missionaries abroad. Before leaving, these missionaries receive at least six months of vigorous training as preparation for their service. In other countries they take secular jobs in line with their vocations and professions for which they have received previous training. They not only support themselves, but also financially back the mission's other spiritual ministries. Pastor Lee visits and ministers to the missionaries on their various fields. Chaeok Chun, who herself was a missionary from Korea to Pakistan, and Marlin Nelson comment on this work in their book *Asian Mission Societies:* "It is one of the rare cases where self-support is working efficiently without workers losing their vision for missionary work. We do think this structure and pattern for foreign mission work is one of the best known and practiced by Asian missions."[3] These self-supporting missionaries concentrate on one-to-one personal evangelism, Bible study in small groups, and the quality of their Christian life and work. Furthermore, they now have started giving support to other missionaries from their fellowship in Third World countries where they cannot earn their own way. This has been begun by sending to Bangladesh a couple who are involved in cross-cultural witness.

As Korean technicians have secured positions abroad, they have started churches among their own people. There are now such evangelical congregations in Iran and Saudi Arabia. In this latter nation, which is the cradle of the Muslim religion, over 20,000 South Koreans are now employed. Some of them have already suffered persecution for their Christian faith. Here again, just as the *diaspora* of Jews around the world has been a testimony to the God of Abraham and Moses, so the scattering of these Third

World believers is proving a witness for the Lord Jesus Christ. However, much more needs to be done to assist these congregations so that they will not only provide worship and witness among their own people, but also will know how to reach the unreached for Christ cross-culturally.

TENTMAKERS IN AND FROM AFRICA

A Christian and his family from the Mar Thoma Church of South India served with the United Nations in Somalia. They had a deep burden for sharing Christ with the Muslims there. One Christmas they invited missionaries, along with Somali Muslim government officials, to their home for an evening of music in which they shared the joys of the season, including a beautiful rendition of "The Messiah." They were thus able to witness to the official stratum of the society there, which the missionaries had been unable to reach.

David Shenk, working with the Mennonite Board in Eastern Africa, writes, "Many Kenyans are being hired to go to Arabia as workmen. The churches in Kenya are attempting to develop seminars to prepare the Christians within these groups of laborers to understand Islam more accurately and to go to Arabia with a sense of mission."

One Nigeran Church has sent out forty missionaries among the Kinuri people. This mission is called the Aquila and Priscilla Movement, since they are self-supporting as they work among the Muslims in that nation. The Evangelical Missionary Society of Nigeria has also sent out around 100 missionary couples who identify with the people among whom they are living by supporting themselves through gardening, vegetable raising, fruit tree growing, poultry producing, tailoring, and merchandising.[4]

PLANS FOR LATIN AMERICAN TENTMAKERS

A Christian from South America writes, "We are hoping to raise up scores of Latins in the coming years to go to the Muslims, especially in the Middle East. Some kind of coordinating system needs to be developed that will . . . list job opportunities in closed countries, challenge students who are just beginning their university studies with this type of mission, keep tabs on all known Christians in closed countries, and hopefully provide some sort of continuing edification ministry to these people who will be so much on their own."

INTERNATIONAL VISITORS
AS POTENTIAL TENTMAKERS

The Scriptures tell us, "Do not forget to entertain strangers, for by so doing some people have entertained angels without knowing it" (Heb. 13:2, NIV). Many Christians in the West are not aware of the strategic missionary opportunity there is with visitors from other nations. For example, government figures show that international travelers to the United States increased from 602,000 in 1960 to 3,674,000 in 1975, over six times as many.[5] There are over 300,000 international students in the United States and Canada as well as many more thousands in European nations. These represent the future leadership of the world, and if they can be reached for Christ they can be his ambassadors in their own countries.

This happened with Gregory the Illuminator. Coming from his native nation of Armenia, he met Christ as a young man while studying in Caesarea. Although the historical facts are not too clear, apparently he traveled back to Armenia in A.D. 287 with the new king, Tiridates III, who had been studying in Rome. When Gregory refused to take part in a heathen sacrifice to the goddess Anahita, the new king became furious and had him tortured and thrown into an underground dungeon to die. He survived only through the kindness of a woman who let food down to him for over thirteen years. When the king got sick, Gregory was brought out of the dungeon to pray for his healing. Tiridates regained his health and through this was converted to the Christian faith. He then vigorously cooperated with Gregory to evangelize the whole country. Idols were destroyed and pagan temples were turned into churches. Thus Armenia became a Christian nation around A.D. 300.[6]

Bakht Singh, an international student who was a Sikh from India, came to Christ in Canada through the witness of a young man in the YMCA at Winnipeg. Since returning to his country, he has led thousands to Christ and has established many worshiping groups of believers throughout the Indian subcontinent.

At an Inter-Varsity sponsored meeting for international students held in a beautiful Christian home in Vancouver, I met an East Indian girl who was studying for her doctor's degree at the University of British Columbia. She said, "I've been to many gatherings where we put on a smile and shake hands, but we keep people at arm's length. Tonight, however, I have felt something different. I have sensed love and want to know what it is. What is the difference between Jesus Christ and other religious teachers?" I mentioned that he not only told us what to do, but that he did it himself. And through his death and resurrection, he gives us forgiveness and the power to live the way we should. She said, "What do you mean by resurrection?" I told her how he had been killed and that the third day he rose again from the dead in his body. She said, "You mean to say that Jesus Christ actually rose from the dead?" When I affirmed this, she earnestly stated, "I have never heard of this before." I then opened the Bible and showed her the account. When I had explained the gospel to her further, I asked whether she wanted to receive him as her Savior. She enthusiastically said, "Yes, by all means!" Today she is a new creation in Christ!

Many of these international students are lonely and discouraged. They are very open to friendship and usually respond more readily to the gospel here than they would in their own countries. They already know the languages and cultures of their areas and thus can be natural tentmakers among their own people. But they must be built up in their faith before returning to their homelands. They also need to be linked up with churches and mission agencies both here and abroad if their witness is to be effective.

Many local evangelical churches have caught the vision of reaching out to these internationals. Christian families befriend them and invite them into their homes. Various mission agencies are also working among students and visitors from the countries where they have work.

God has also raised up parachurch organizations with special ministries to these internationals. The Inter-Varsity Christian Fellowship works among these students from abroad. One organization which specializes in this strategic work is International Students Incorporated. They have a program of welcoming students as they arrive from abroad, helping them with their adjustments, introducing them to Christian families and churches, inviting them to conferences over vacations, and supplying them with Scripture portions in their own languages.

Campus Crusade has a division for this called the International Student Ministry. In spite of the fine work that these organizations are doing, the numbers of visitors are so great and the opportunities are so vast that far more needs to be done in this area if full advantage is to be taken of this unprecedented challenge.

Communists are very much aware of the strategic nature of these students. They actively recruit them in countries all over the world and seek to win them for their ideology. Chou En-lai became a Communist while he was a student in France. Ho Chi Minh as a young man worked in Boston washing dishes in the Parker House Hotel, only a few steps from evangelical Christian churches, but was not reached for Christ. Later he too became a Communist in France. An Afghan student told me that he had become an atheistic materialist at an American university. If we Christians do not wake up, these very ones whom we have not welcomed in Jesus' name will later rise up to oppose the Lord and those who bear his name.

Recently the local church we attend entertained international students for a weekend. The one who stayed with us was a Muslim from Mecca studying at Harvard. No Christians are allowed to go to that city, which is the religious center of Islam, but God brought this student from there right into our home. It was a thrill to hear Christian students from Africa witnessing to him about their faith in Jesus Christ.

With these international visitors, let us obey the admonition of the Scriptures: "If a stranger lives with you in your land, you should not mistreat him. But the stranger living with you should be treated as one who is born among you. You should love him as yourself" (Lev. 19:33, 34). As we take this admonition seriously, many will find the Lord as Savior and return to their lands as tentmakers for Christ.

20/TWELVE TYPES OF TENTMAKERS TODAY

The latest *Mission Handbook*[1] lists the total number of overseas Protestant missionary personnel from North America at 53,494. The previous edition of the same survey volume records the numbers in 1975 at 35,458.[2] This is a 50 percent increase in personnel, for which we can truly give praise to God. Many more fully supported workers still need to be recruited and sent out. Nevertheless, approximately half of the people of the world who as yet have not been reached with the gospel live in areas where traditional missionaries are not allowed. How can these be evangelized? One way to reach them is through "tentmaking" missions. Just as the term "missionary" can mean either a Christian in general or a special cross-cultural witness, in the same way the term "tentmaker" can refer to many different categories of believers. These fall into twelve groups:

1. Lay Christians at home. The Bible teaches about "the priesthood of the believers" in Revelation 1:6 and 5:10. This reveals that Christians like the Old Testament priests not only have a relationship to God but also a responsibility to others. Jesus Christ said, "You are witnesses" (Luke 24:48) and this applies to all Christians. But Dr. James Kennedy states that 95 percent of believers never witness for their faith and only 2 percent ever lead another person to Christ. Thus lay people need to be encouraged, trained, and involved in personal evangelism if the whole world is to be reached.

2. The believer at home who is engaged in cross-cultural witness with international students, foreign visitors, refugees from other countries, and local ethnic groups. Such witnesses are self-supporting "foreign" missionaries at home. International Students Inc., Campus Crusade, and Inter-Varsity can assist in putting you in touch with students and visitors from abroad. (See addresses in appendix.)

3. Those who have gone abroad for cross-cultural witness with a regular mission board but who have secured a secular position such as teaching in a university. Not only is this a help to the financial situation of the mission, but also at times it enables a person to get a visa from the host government which otherwise might be difficult to obtain. William Carey was a model of this type of tentmaker. He first went as a missionary who was supported by churches in England, but later he became self-supporting by working with an indigo factory and also teaching Sanskrit in a government college. More recently, a missionary couple who had served in Japan for twenty-two years could not raise the high support figure needed to return to the field. They have gone back as salaried English teachers in a government program while still being associated with their mission. And they are able to use the New Testament as a teaching text.

4. Christians who have trained and planned to go overseas as self-supporting cross-cultural witnesses. This type of ministry has great possibilities in China today where regular missionaries are not allowed to stay but where they welcome technicians, teachers, scientists, and business people who will help that nation in its development. The Overseas Counseling Service and Intercristo (addresses in appendix) can assist in advising and referring qualified people for such positions.

5. Earnest Christian students who have been trained in witness through their churches, Campus Crusade, International Students Inc., Inter-Varsity, the Navigators, Young Life, Youth for Christ, and other organizations. Some of these are studying in universities around the world and are finding wide openings as student tentmakers. Recently on a trip to the People's Republic of China, my wife and I met a fine Christian girl studying there. But she was the only believer among more than 500 international students who had come to the university where she was working. Having already led some former Communists to

Christ, she longed to have other Christian students join her in China.

6. *Teachers.* Many foreign governments are ready and willing to pay for the transportation and salaries of English teachers who will come to assist with language instruction. There are also opportunities for teachers of other subjects. A young Christian engineer recently took a tour to China. She was offered and accepted a contract to teach engineering at a university in the People's Republic.

7. *Christian retirees.* They can assist greatly with their expertise and experience abroad, especially in advisory capacities. Ruth Siemens states, "seven thousand Americans have retired in Poland where they receive special privileges. Five thousand live in Yugoslavia, four thousand in France, six thousand on the sunny coast of Spain, seventeen thousand in Germany, and fifty thousand in Italy! Others are in Latin America. Some have retired in Sri Lanka! Sometimes their retirement income will stretch further. And their long experience can be put to good use. Older missionaries are needed in countries where age is held in great respect."[3]

8. *Short term service abroad.* Students who pay their own way to go abroad for summer service, professionals such as doctors and nurses who offer their services free to mission hospitals, and those who go on one- or two-year short term service assignments could be included in this category. For example, the Mormons use this type of missionary service. They have more than 26,000 young people at any one time who serve for two years at their own expense.

9. *Positions in international business.* One way to help overcome injustices of certain multinational corporations is to get Christians in them who can influence decisions and policies. For example, Sir Frederick Catherwood, the son-in-law of well-known Bible expositor Dr. Martyn Lloyd-Jones, has drawn up an ethical code and is seeking to get international companies to subscribe to it.

10. *Christians serving abroad with embassies, military missions, the Peace Corps, a branch of the United Nations, or other such official organizations.* There are also many voluntary agencies that have work overseas with which Christians can get positions. Such jobs afford opportunities for service in relief,

education, public health, and development. Beside the many
secular agencies in this field, there are evangelical organizations
such as World Vision, World Relief Corporation, World
Concern, Food for the Hungry, Compassion, and other
ministries that need workers.

*11. Christians who plant expatriate churches around the
world.* Not only are there English-speaking congregations, but
Christians from other language groups have also started
churches abroad. Korean believers have begun many new
congregations in countries where they have gone. The pastors of
these expatriate churches are tentmakers in a real sense since
they usually are supported by the congregations which they
serve. The International Fellowship of Christians seeks to assist
English-speaking pastors with the securing of positions in
churches around the world, as does the Program for Churchmen
Overseas (see appendix for addresses).

Ford Madison, a Christian tentmaker in Central America, in
speaking at the Lausanne Congress stated, "Does the layman fit
anywhere into world evangelism? What about the millions of
ordinary Christians? What do laymen want? We want to be
involved in what really counts . . . how to study the Bible, how
to pray, how to live in love, how to witness, how to have Christ
formed in us . . . that we too might be personally involved in
world evangelization."[4]

*12. Internationals who come to Christ and then return to their
own countries as Christian laymen and laywomen who can be
witnesses to their own people.* International Students Inc. and
other organizations, as previously mentioned, are seeking to
train believers from abroad as well as ones who come to the
Lord so that they will be effective witnesses when they return to
their own nations. These can help plant churches in Third
World nations along with mission structures which can send
witnesses to unreached people in their countries as well as
throughout the world.

All of the various types of tentmakers need assistance from
local churches and from mission agencies if they are to be
effective. To meet this need, TEAM has now decided to train
tentmakers along with their regular candidates. Also, S.I.M.
International has started a division to assist tentmakers with
getting positions in Africa. The Evangelical Foreign Missions

Association (EFMA) and the Interdenominational Foreign
Missions Association (IFMA) have held a joint conference for
personnel secretaries where they considered tentmaking
opportunities and their relationship to mission agencies.
Furthermore, many local churches are including the challenge of
tentmaking in their missionary conferences. This is very
important; if tentmakers are to be successful communicators of
the gospel, they need the prayer backing and interest of local
congregations.

Let us pray that we as Christians today may not only affirm
the biblical principle of "the priesthood of the believers," but
that we may put it into practice through tentmaking. An Afghan
saying states that "where water has once flowed, it can flow
again." The great spiritual awakenings in history have involved
Christian lay people as well as members of the clergy. Our Lord
Jesus Christ promised, "He that believeth in me, as the
Scripture hath said, out of his belly shall flow rivers of living
water" (John 7:38). If "God's frozen assets" of lay believers can
have their hearts strangely warmed and melted by the Holy
Spirit, then "the earth shall be filled with the knowledge of the
glory of the Lord, as the waters cover the sea" (Habakkuk 2:14).

21/FUTURE STRATEGY

Send us around the world with the news of your saving power and your eternal plan for mankind. . . . And peoples from remotest lands will worship him (Psa. 67:2, 7, TLB).

"Without lay people involved in world evangelism," writes missions executive William Kerr of C.&M.A., "the task will never be completed." One can see how this is true today, especially with mainland China opening up to Christian tentmakers. But the question arises, "How can the ministry of self-supporting witnesses be made more effective so that they can become a deciding factor in worldwide evangelization?"

Margaret Mitchell, an American who served in Iran, observes, "The major problem of the tentmaker is that he/she has no support structure. An agency or subagency under another organization would be fantastic." In regard to the possibility of establishing such a support structure, John Bennett of the Association of Church Missions Committees states that there are "few ideas with greater potential than the establishment of an agency to facilitate self-supporting witness." Andrew Dymond, who is associated with the Bible and Medical Missionary Fellowship, states, "There will be an ever increasing number of self-supporting Christians. There needs to be the implementation of an effective infrastructure for tentmaking witness."[1]

We thank God for various agencies who have worked in this strategic area. We have seen how Overseas Counseling Service has established an office in Seattle for this very purpose of assisting Christian students and graduates with assignments abroad. We have also noted Campus Crusade's Agape Program, which is training and locating dedicated workers overseas. Furthermore Wayne Shabaz, in conjunction with Missionary Internship, has established a Christian agency for recruiting and training personnel to go abroad with multinational corporations. Various mission boards have developed programs to incorporate self-supporting witnesses into their field strategies. But if, as Waldron Scott of the World Evangelical Fellowship states, tentmaking ministries are to be "the next great creative movement that God's Spirit is going to bring into existence in missionary effort," there needs to be more coordination. He further states, "I believe that somewhere in the next five years God is going to raise up a major new missionary agency that devotes itself exclusively to servicing laymen who are witnessing overseas." Such a structure would cooperate with the organizations, mission boards, and Third World agencies which already have tentmaking ministries.

Phil Parshall of Bangladesh comments, "It would be good if an IFMA-EFMA sponsored organization could be formed to deal with recruiting and orienting lay people toward service abroad. This group could link the tentmakers to an appropriate mission in the country where they will reside. It is important for the layman to coordinate his activities with the local evangelical missionaries."

Brother Andrew wrote, in relation to the preparation of this book on self-supporting witness, "The reason why I think your work is so important is that so far nothing has been done which is thoroughly coordinated. There may be some doubts as to whether international coordination would be a wise move because of the enemy's counterattack that will undoubtedly come. If there is anything definite I can do, let me know." This brought back to mind a statement which he made to us when he visited Afghanistan trying to discover ways of getting Scriptures into closed bordering areas. He warned, "If we do not go to the world with the gospel, it will come against us in judgment."

If a coordinating organization were formed to assist tentmakers, what would be its functions? For one thing, it could assist in much-needed recruitment for tentmaking. It could provide information along with the opportunities that are open for service. Also, it could direct and assist in the preparation and orientation of tentmakers. Dr. Ted Engstrom, the executive vice-president of

World Vision, has written, "It sounds as if you are tackling a very
worthwhile venture designed to help tentmakers overseas.
Cross-cultural instruction might unleash thousands of earnest
Christians toward a highly effective witness for our Lord." Such
an organization could also work in conjunction with mission
agencies, seminaries, Christian colleges and universities, Bible
institutes, and parachurch movements in training for effective
tentmaking service. It could provide job matching facilities and
give assistance in placement. It could link tentmakers with mission
boards that work in the areas where they were going.

Such an organization could sensitize local congregations to
appreciate the great potential there is in the work of
self-supporting missionaries. As Phill Butler of Intercristo has
said, "When was the last time you heard from your pulpit Sunday
morning, 'Let's pray for Charlie Jones, our missionary with Shell
Oil in Caracas'? The idea that a person can function in the
commercial, military, or government arena overseas as a
missionary . . . is largely overlooked if not discredited in our
churches. This myopic view of Christian service has seriously
stunted the Church's growth worldwide. It has blinded us in our
ability to mount an effective Great Commission campaign under
the headship of our Lord Jesus Christ. Local churches should
view these self-supporting individuals as real missionaries—worthy
of all the prayer and other benefits flowing from the local
fellowship. These are positions which do not require massive sums
for our local congregations to fund. The present status of things
demands that we look for additional ways to thrust forth
laborers."[2]

Such an agency could also encourage Christian students to
enroll in universities around the world where they could acquire
language skills and become culturally oriented while they
witnessed for Christ. This would also prepare them for possible
future service in that area. Such an organization could encourage
research on countries and peoples to discover needs for
development and to seek to provide these through tentmakers.
Moreover, this organization could work on a global strategy for
incorporating tentmakers into the total picture of worldwide
evangelization. Even as Dr. Kenneth Strachan, the architect of
Evangelism-in-Depth, stated, "The successful fulfillment of the
Great Commission lies in the mobilization of every Christian, for
the expansion of any movement is in direct proportion to its

success in mobilizing its membership for continuous propagation of its beliefs."[3] Challenging and encouraging all Christian tentmakers to be effective witnesses right along with fully-supported missionaries can be the key to the evangelization of the world.

Such a structure could work out ways of sending and equipping tentmakers to help evangelize where regular missionaries are not allowed. Ed Dayton, head of the MARC division of World Vision, states, "The fact of the matter is that thirty-eight countries with a [total] population of 1,993,600,000 permit no foreign missionaries of any type or greatly restrict any evangelists within their countries."[4] These areas are off limits to regular mission work, and if they are to be reached it must be done in other ways.

Such an agency could keep tabs on and assist all known self-supporting missionaries around the world. It could also help put them in touch with expatriate and national churches. Dr. Donald McGavran has suggested that a mission also is needed to assist with planting English-speaking churches all over the world in places where they are needed.

Such an organization could facilitate tentmakers with linguistic and language learning opportunities. It could provide seminars on the field to assist with specific areas of need, and it could help tentmakers with effective evangelism. It could provide ways for conserving their converts and could tie their work in with ongoing mission strategy. It could publish materials for self-supporting witnesses which would give them assistance on the field, and could also carry on correspondence with them regarding immediate needs.

Such an agency could send roving delegates to oversee, encourage, and edify tentmakers on the field. It could assist with governmental problems and relations. Self-supporting witnesses who make good salaries could contribute to a fund to aid those who have special financial needs and to help cover the expenses of the coordinating agency. It could debrief the tentmakers following their service abroad and thus collect and use valuable information which might otherwise be lost. And it could help cushion their reentry home through reorientation programs.

But how is such an organization to be established? Phill Butler suggests that possibly a conference should be called on this subject which would bring together interested parties, both denominational and interdenominational. He states, "We here at

Intercristo would certainly be glad to work on such a project, maybe more as coordinator than sponsor, although we would be glad I'm sure to take whatever role the Lord might lead us to in the matter." Ken Nolin, who has worked as a missionary in Egypt, writes regarding the possibility of such an agency, "The opportunities opened by this are mind-boggling. If only we can take advantage of it all quietly, without undue publicity so that we do not jeopardize what's being done." This warning regarding needless fanfare should be well taken.

Sir Kenneth Grubb, a missions statesman both in his associations with World Dominion and the Church Missionary Society of England, writes, "It is conceivable that eventually there would be a worldwide fellowship of lay people working outside their own countries. If I could live my career over again, I think I would give much of my time to this task."[5] William Carey, that great missionary and tentmaker, before he went to India to initiate the modern missionary movement, preached a telling sermon with the theme, "Expect great things from God and attempt great things for God." He based this message on a prophetic text which should also be God's Word to tentmakers today. "Enlarge the place of your tent, stretch your tent curtains wide, do not hold back; lengthen your cords, strengthen your stakes. For you will spread out to the right and to the left; your descendants will dispossess nations and settle in their desolate cities" (Isa. 54:2, 3, NIV). "For the earth shall be full of the knowledge of the Lord, as the waters cover the sea" (Isa. 11:9). And in this way may the Lord's Prayer, which he taught us, be fulfilled, "Thy kingdom come. Thy will be done on earth" (Matt. 6:10).

NOTES

Chapter 2, An Unprecendented Opportunity

1. Dr. Waldron Scott stated this before the National Conference of the Association of Church Missions Committees at Wheaton, Illinois, in August 1977, as he was speaking on "The Student Missions Movement." A cassette tape of this message can be secured from A.C.M.C., P.O. Box ACMC, Wheaton, Illinois 60189.
2. Herbert Kane, *Understanding Christian Missions*. (Grand Rapids, MI: Baker, 1975), p. 405.
3. Canon Max A.C. Warren, *Missions Under the Cross*. Norman Goodall, ed. (London: Edinburgh House, 1953), p. 31.
4. Roland Allen. *The Ministry of the Spirit*. London: World Dominion Press, 1960), p. 65.
5. In Matthew 28:19 the Greek words $\tau\grave{\alpha}\ \overset{\prime\prime}{\epsilon}\theta\nu\eta$ are used, which can be translated "ethnic groups." This term is also used in Rev. 5:9 and 7:9.
6. Roland Allen, Sir Kenneth Grubb, Professor Herbert Kane, and others have used the term "non-professional missionary" in their books and writings.
7. Eric Fife and Arthur Glasser. *Missions in Crisis*. (Downers Grove, IL: InterVarsity Press, 1961), pp. 163-165.
8. Dr. R. Pierce Beaver and others use the expression "the lay apostolate" for "tentmakers."
9. Mr. Emmett McKowen, who taught as a Christian in Afghanistan and then worked for many years with the United States Information Agency, has suggested this term, "lay pastor." He referred to himself as this and found that it was accepted and understood by non-Christian colleagues.
10. This is the expression used in an address given at the Urbana Student Missionary Convention in 1973. This material is published in *Jesus Christ: Lord of the Universe, Hope of the World*. David Howard, ed. (Downers Grove, IL: InterVarsity, 1974).
11. Edward R. Dayton, ed. *Mission Handbook: North American Protestant Ministries Overseas*, 11th ed. (Monrovia, CA: MARC of World Vision, 1976), p. 26.
12. Herbert Kane. *Winds of Change in the Christian Mission*. Chicago: Moody Press, 1973, 1973), p. 177.
13. Andrew Dymond. BMMF. Quadrennial Report. Karachi, Pakistan, 1978.
14. "Travelers Going Abroad," *U.S. News and World Report*, 18 July 1977.

15. U.S. Dept. of Commerce, Bureau of Census. *Statistical Abstract of the U.S., 1976.* (Washington D.C.: Government Printing Press, 1976), p. 223.
16. *The World Almanac and Book of Facts 1978.* (New York: Newspaper Enterprise Association, 1977), p. 606.
17. The reason for the discrepancy between the number of people going abroad increasing tenfold and the number of passports issued increasing just ninefold is that often one passport is issued for a couple or for an entire family.
18. *The World Almanac,* p. 606.
19. Eugene W. Grubbs. "What Are Southern Baptist Laymen Doing Overseas?" *The Commission.* (Richmond, VA: Foreign Mission Board of the Southern Baptist Convention, January, 1974), p. 4.
20. Stephen Neill. *A History of Christian Missions.* (Middlesex, England: Penguin, 1975), p. 559.
21. James Kennedy. *Evangelism Explosion.* (Wheaton, IL: Tyndale House, 1970), p. 1.
22. J.D. Douglas, ed. *Let The Earth Hear His Voice.* (Minneapolis, MN: World Wide Publications, 1975), p. 5.

Chapter 3, The Imprimatur of Scripture

1. It has been said that this book influenced missions the way Martin Luther's "Ninety-Five Theses" affected the Reformation. William Carey's publication has also been called the "Magna Carta" of Christian missions.
2. William Carey. *An Enquiry Into the Obligations of Christians to Use Means for the Conversion of the Heathens.* (Leicester, England: Ann Ireland, 1792), p. 9, (hereafter cited as *Enquiry*).
3. *Ibid.,* pp. 7, 68.
4. Neill, *A History of Christian Missions,* p. 24.

Chapter 4, The History of Tentmaking

1. John Stewart. *The Nestorian Missionary Enterprise: A Church on Fire.* (Edinburgh, Scotland: Clarke, 1923), p. 34.
2. *Ibid.,* p. 18.
3. *Ibid.,* p. 47.
4. *Ibid.,* p. 198.
5. *Ibid.,* Introduction, p. 29.
6. *Ibid.,* pp. 37, 38.
7. Stephen Neill. *Studies in Church History,* p. 152. (This book was republished under the title, *A History of Christian Missions.* See above.)
8. August J. Kling. "Columbus—A Layman 'Christ-bearer' to Uncharted Isles," *The Presbyterian Layman,* October 1971, p. 4.
9. William J. Danker. *Profit for the Lord.* (Grand Rapids, MI: Eerdmans, 1971), p. 5.
10. Neill, *A History of Christian Missions,* p. 232.
11. David Bentley-Taylor. *My Love Must Wait: The Story of Henry Martyn.* (Downers Grove, IL: InterVarsity Press, 1975), p. 50.
12. John Thiessen. *A Survey of World Missions.* (Downers Grove, IL: InterVarsity Press, 1956), p. 21.
13. Danker, *Profit for the Lord,* p. 17.
14. *Ibid.,* p. 60.
15. *Ibid.,* p. 55.
16. *Ibid.,* p. 52.
17. *Ibid.,* p. 73.
18. John Seamands. *The Supreme Task of the Church.* (Grand Rapids, MI: Eerdmans, 1964), p. 73.
19. Neill, *A History of Christian Missions,* p. 263.

20. Sir Kenneth Grubb. *The Need for Non-Professional Missionaries.* (London: World Dominion Press, 1931), p. 11.
21. Neill, *A History of Christian Missions,* p. 291.
22. Justin Perkins. *Missionary Life in Persia.* (Boston, MA: American Tract Society, 1861), pp. 87, 88.
23. H. B. T. Holland. *No Second Spring?* (London: C.M.S., 1951), p. 15.
24. Robert Clark. *The Missions of the C.M.S. and C.E.Z.M.S. in the Punjab and Sindh.* (London: C.M.S., 1904), p. 177.
25. *Ibid.,* pp. 178, 179.
26. *The Second Report of the Mission to the Afghans at Peshawar, 1856–1859.* (London: C.M.S.), p. 25.
27. Danker, *Profit for the Lord,* pp. 87–89.
28. *Ibid.,* p. 121.
29. Neill, *A History of Christian Missions,* pp. 327, 328.
30. Roberta H. Winter. *Once More Around Jericho.* (Pasadena, CA: William Carey Library, 1978), p. 194.
31. Jenny de Mayer. *Adventures with God.* (Toronto, Canada: Evangelical Publishers, 1942).

Chapter 5, Tentmaking by Non-Christians
1. Dick Van Halsema. *Missionary Monthly,* June-July 1977.
2. *The Church Around the World,* vol. 7, no. 5. (Wheaton, IL: Tyndale House, April 1977), p. 2.
3. Edward Dayton, ed., *Mission Handbook,* 11th ed., p. 29.
4. *Ibid.*

Chapter 6, The Spirit Told Me to Go
1. At present there are over 100 staff workers with International Students, Inc., and its headquarters is located at Star Ranch, Box C, Colorado Springs, CO 80901.

Chapter 7, After You, Marco Polo
1. This was the title of an article in *The National Geographic* telling of a trip the Shors took through Afghanistan.

Chapter 8, A Wonderful Country Ahead
1. Seventeen from these two churches have either served the Lord in Afghanistan or have visited for prolonged periods. The First Presbyterian Church in Schenectady ever since has kindly continued to keep me in the position of "Pastor Extra Muros" or "Minister Outside Walls."
2. Frank Laubach. *World Literacy Newsletter,* Vol. 4, No. 4, 1951, p. 2.

Chapter 10, Tentmakers Today
1. Arthur D. Iliff. "Missions on the Borders of Afghanistan," Margaret W. Haines, ed. Philadelphia, PA, July 1942, p. 4.
2. Joseph Newman. *People Helping People.* (Washington D.C.: U.S. Volunteers in Action, U.S. News and World Report Books, 1971), pp. 16, 18.
3. Marcia Sayre. *Research for Mission Strategy in Iran.* (Upper Darby, PA: BMMF, 1976), p. 18.
4. Cathy Phelps. *The Guide to Moving Overseas.* (Box 236, Lamont, PA: privately published, 1978).

Chapter 11, Tentmaking Makes Sense
1. Nate Krupp. *A World to Win.* (Minneapolis, MN: Bethany Fellowship, 1966), Foreword.

2. Ross Kinsler. "Bases for Change in Theology of Education," *Latin American Pulse,* August 1977.
3. Grubb, *The Need for Non-Professional Missionaries,* p. 67.
4. Neill, *A History of Christian Missions,* p. 43.
5. Allen, *The Ministry of the Spirit,* pp. 78, 79.
6. Roland Allen. *The Spontaneous Expansion of the Church.* (Grand Rapids, MI: Eerdmans, 1973), p. 117.
7. Sir Kenneth Grubb. *Frontier,* Vol. 4, No. 4, Winter, 1961, p. 238.
8. Hendrik Kraemer. *A Theology of the Laity.* (Philadelphia: Westminster Press, 1958), pp. 9, 10.
9. *Ibid.,* p. 153.
10. *Ibid.,* p. 45.
11. *Ibid.,* pp. 28, 45.
12. Howard Mattsson-Boze. "Self-Supporting Missionaries: Problems and Opportunities," written for IVCF, 1977.
13. Angus I. Kinnear. *Against the Tide: The Story of Watchman Nee.* (Eastbourne, England: Victory Press, 1973), pp. 126–135.
14. Peter C. Wagner. *Stop the World I Want to Get On.* (Glendale, CA: Gospel Light, 1974), p. 62.
15. Mattsson-Boze, "Self-Supporting Missionaries."
16. Kane, *Understanding Christian Missions,* p. 390.
17. Kane, *Winds of Change in Christian Mission,* pp. 123, 124.
18. *Ibid.,* p. 125.
19. *Goal,* Vol. 11, No. 3. (Upper Darby, PA: BMMF, 1978), p. 11.
20. Donald McGavran. "The Genesis and Strategy of the Homogeneous Unit Principle." A paper delivered at the Lausanne Theology and Education group consultation on the Homogeneous Unit Principle, Fuller Theological Seminary, Pasadena, CA, 31 May—2 June 1977.
21. Theodore Pennell. *Among the Wild Tribes of the Afghan Frontier.* (London: Seeley, 1909), p. 299.
22. Flora Davidson. *Hidden Highway.* (Sterling, Scotland: Tract Enterprise, 1944), p. 136.
23. Douglas, *Let the Earth Hear His Voice,* p. 6.
24. Phillip Butler. "Missionaries: How to Bring Them In," *Advent Christian Missions,* November 1977, pp. 6, 7.
25. Adams Mangone, and Cleveland. *The Overseas American.* (New York: McGraw Hill, 1960), p. 97.
26. Danker, *Profit for the Lord,* p. 139.

Chapter 12, Tentmaking Students Abroad
1. Bruce Bell. "Where the Action Isn't," *Christianity Today,* 7 October 1977, p. 29.
2. Douglas, *Let the Earth Hear His Voice,* p. 759.
3. Waldron Scott. "The Student Missions Movement." An address given at the Association of Church Missions Committees in Wheaton, IL, 1977.
4. Kane, *Winds of Change in the Christian Mission,* p. 142.
5. From the Muslim Students' Association of the United States and Canada Calendar for 1398–1978, p. 2. P.O. Box 38, Plainfield, IN 46168.
6. *Ibid.,* pp. 18–20.
7. "Exchange of Students," *U.S. News and World Report,* 18 July 1977.
8. Mrs. Howard Taylor. *Behind the Ranges, Fraser of Lisuland.* (London: Lutterworth, 1944), p. 191.
9. Dayton, *Mission Handbook,* p. 21.
10. "MIT, Harvard Students to Study in China," *The Boston Globe,* 5 December 1978, p. 25.
11. Michael C. Griffiths. *Give Up Your Small Ambitions.* (Chicago: Moody Press, 1972), p. 4.

Chapter 13, Investing Yourself for Christ
1. Margaret Nash. *Christians—World Citizens.* (London: Edinburgh House, 1965), p. 31.
2. Mattsson-Boze, "Self-Supporting Missionary," p. 31.
3. Chua Wee Hian. "An IFES Overview: Past, Present and Future," *Branch,* IVCF, 1 September 1977, p. 3.
4. Kane, *Understanding Christian Missions,* p. 388.
5. Kane, *Winds of Change in the Christian Mission,* p. 148.
6. Sayre, *Research for Mission Strategy in Iran,* pp. 20, 30.
7. Nash, *Christians—World Citizens,* p. 31.
8. *The Mission Handbook* published by MARC of World Vision lists nations abroad with all the North American Protestant mission agencies working in each. *The Mission Handbook* of the U.S. Catholic Mission Council (1302 Eighteenth St., N.W., Suite 702, Washington D.C. 20036) lists the countries where Catholic missions are working.
9. John T. Semands. *Around the World for Christ.* (Wilmore, KY: private publication, 1973), pp. 115, 116.
10. From the leaflet "Unofficial Missionaries," published by the Foreign Mission Board of the Southern Baptist Convention, 3806 Monument Ave., Richmond, VA 23230.
11. Kane, *Winds of Change in Christian Mission,* pp. 137, 138.

Chapter 14, The Crucial Position of Mission Boards
1. Ralph Winter. *Grounds for a New Thrust in World Mission.* (Pasadena, CA: William Carey Library, 1977), p. 2.
2. Ralph Winter. "Who Are the Three Billion?" *Church Growth Bulletin,* Vol. 13, No. 6, July 1977, p. 141.
3. Danker, *Profit for the Lord,* p. 136.
4. Quoted from the findings of the Bible and Medical Missionary Fellowship Quadrennial held in Pakistan and India in 1978.
5. Robert Kurtz. "The Lay-Worker as a New Type of Missionary," *The International Review of Missions,* Vol. 42, No. 167, July 1953, p. 314.
6. *Ibid.,* p. 308.
7. Kane, *Winds of Change in Christian Mission,* p. 119.
8. Mattsson-Boze, "Self-Supporting Missionary."
9. Stanley E. Anderson. *The American Scientific Affiliation Newsletter,* February-March, 1978.
10. Mattsson-Boze, "The Self-Supporting Missionary."
11. From the leaflet "Go C.S.O.," World Evangelism Crusade, Box A, Fort Washington, PA 19034.
12. Kane, *Winds of Change in Christian Mission,* p. 123.

Chapter 15, Preparation and Orientation
1. Danker, *Profit for the Lord,* p. 130.
2. Phill Butler. "The Self-Supporting Missionary—Another Look," *Intercristo.*
3. From a report by Andrew Dymond at the BMMF Quadrennial held in Karachi and New Delhi, March 1978.
4. Kane, *Understanding Christian Missions,* p. 405.
5. Kinnear, *Against the Tide,* pp. 168–180.
6. McGavran, Donald. *The Clash Between Christianity and Cultures.* (Washington D.C.: Canon Press, 1974), p. 41.

Chapter 16, Life Abroad
1. Kane, *Winds of Change in Christian Mission,* p. 104.
2. Grubb, "Layman Abroad," p. 236.
3. *Ibid.,* p. 238.

4. Ruth Siemens, The Seminar on Self-Supporting Witness: The Urbana Missionary Convention, December 1976.
5. Griffiths, *Give Up Your Small Ambitions*, p. 118.

Chapter 17, English-Language Churches Abroad
1. Neill, *A History of Christian Missions*, p. 226.
2. KCCC trustees have included: Jordan Churchill, Jim Cudney, Elmer Engstrom, Ernest Gordon, Littleton Groom, Margaret Haines, Howard Larsen, William Miller, Tom Niblock, Tim Roberts, Cleo Shook and Christy Wilson, Sr.
3. Grubbs, "Southern Baptist Laymen," p. 5.
4. SBC Pamphlet. "Know Your Baptist Missions," (Richmond, VA: SBC, 1977), inside cover.
5. SBC Pamphlet. "Scattered Abroad: English-Language Work Overseas," (Richmond VA: SBC, 1973), p. 1.

Chapter 18, Witness While You Work
1. Carey, *Enquiry*, p. 75.
2. T. Stanley Soltau. *Missions at the Crossroads*. (Wheaton, IL: Van Kampen, 1954), pp. 44, 45.
3. James and Marti Hefley. *Uncle Cam*. (Waco, TX: Word, 1974).
4. James F. Engel and H. Wilbert Norton. *What's Gone Wrong With the Harvest?* (Grand Rapids, MI: Zondervan, 1976), pp. 43–56.
5. Douglas, *Let the Earth Hear His Voice*, p. 7.
6. Nash, *Christians—World Citizens*, p. 19.
7. Mattsson-Boze, "Self-Supporting Missionary."

Chapter 19, Third World Tentmakers
1. Marlin A. Nelson and Chaeok Chun. *Asian Mission Societies: New Resources for World Evangelization*. (Monrovia, CA: World Vision's MARC, 1976), p. 18.
2. Douglas, *Let the Earth Hear His Voice*, p. 6.
3. Nelson and Chun, *Asian Mission Societies*, pp. 64, 65.
4. Wagner, *Stop the World*, pp. 111, 112.
5. U.S. Bureau of Economic Analysis. Survey of Current Business. These figures exclude Canadians and Mexicans.
6. Harold R. Cook. *Historic Patterns of Church Growth*. (Chicago, IL: Moody Press, 1971), pp. 19–21.

Chapter 20, Twelve Types of Tentmakers Today
1. Wilson, Samuel. *Mission Handbook: North American Protestant Ministries Overseas*. (Monrovia, CA: MARC, World Vision, 1981), 12th edition.
2. Dayton, Edward. *Mission Handbook: North American Protestant Ministries Overseas*. (Monrovia, CA: MARC, World Vision, 1976), 11th edition.
3. Siemens, Ruth. "The Professional and The Tentmaker," *Impact*, Wheaton, IL: C.B.F.M.S., May, 1981, p. 12.
4. Douglas, J. D., ed. *Let The Earth Hear His Voice*. Madison, Ford, "A Layman Looks at World Evangelization." (Minneapolis, MN: World Wide, 1975), pp. 457-458.

Chapter 21, Future Strategy
1. Andrew Dymond in a report to the BMMF Quadrennial held in Karachi and New Delhi, March 1978.
2. Butler, "The Self-Supporting Missionary—Another Look."
3. Kenneth R. Strachan. *The Inescapable Calling*. (Grand Rapids, MI: Eerdmans, 1968), pp. 113, 114.
4. EdDayton,ed.*MARC Newsletter*. (Monrovia, CA: World Vision, September, 1978).
5. Grubb, "Layman Abroad," p. 237.

BIBLIOGRAPHY/BOOKS

Allen, Roland. *The Case for Voluntary Clergy.* London: Eyre & Sotiswade, 1930.
_____. *The Ministry of the Spirit.* London: World Dominion Press, 1960.
_____. *Missionary Methods: St. Paul's or Ours?* Grand Rapids, MI: Eerdmans, 1962.
_____. *The Spontaneous Expansion of the Church.* Grand Rapids, MI: Eerdmans, 1973.
Angel, Juvenal L. *American Encyclopedia of International Information.* New York: World Trade Academy Press, 1972. Vols. I–X.
Arnold, T. W. *The Preaching of Islam: A History of the Propagation of the Muslim Faith.* London: Constable, 1913.
Ayers, Francis O. *The Ministry of the Laity.* Philadelphia: Westminster Press, 1962.
Beaver, R. Pierce. *The Missionary Between the Times.* Garden City: Doubleday & Co., 1968.
Bentley-Taylor, David. *My Love Must Wait, The Story of Henry Martyn.* Downers Grove, IL: InterVarsity Press, 1975.
Bergstedt, Alan W. *Scripture Translation Information Bank* (Status of Bible Translation—Western Hemisphere). Final Advance of Scripture Translation, 1740 Westminster Drive, Denton, TX 76201, 1972.
Braun, Neil. *Laity Mobilized.* Grand Rapids: Eerdmans, 1971.
Carey, William. *An Enquiry into the Obligations of Christians to Use Means for the Conversion of the Heathens.* Leicester, England: Ann Ireland, 1792. (Reprinted London: Hodder & Stoughton, 1891.)
Chang, Lit-sen. *Strategy of Missions in the Orient.* Presbyterian & Reformed Publishing Co., 1970.
Clark, Dennis E. *The Third World & Mission.* Waco: Word Books, 1971.
Clark, Robert. *The Missions of C.M.S. and C.E.Z.M.S. in the Punjab and Sindh.* London: C.M.S., 1904.
Cleveland, Harlan and Mangone, Gerald. *The Art of Overseasmanship.* Syracuse: Syracuse University Press, 1957.
Cleveland; Mangone; Adams. *The Overseas American.* New York: McGraw Hill, 1960.
Collins, Marjorie A. *Manual For Accepted Missionary Candidates.* Pasadena, CA: William Carey Library, 1972.

Cook, Harold R. *Historic Patterns of Church Growth.* Chicago: Moody, 1971.

Covell, R. R. & Wagner, C. P. *An Extension Seminary Primer.* Pasadena: William Carey Library, 1971.

Crosby, Barbara & Smyth, Stuart J. *U.S. Non-Profit Organizations in Development Assistance Abroad.* Technical Assistance Information Clearing House of the American Council of Voluntary Agencies for Foreign Service, Inc., 200 Park Avenue South, New York, NY 10003.

Danker, William. *Profit for the Lord.* Grand Rapids, MI: Eerdmans, 1971.

Davidson, Flora. *Hidden Highway.* Sterling, Scotland: Tract Enterprise, 1944.

Dayton, Edward R., ed. *Mission Handbook: North American Protestant Ministries Overseas,* 11th ed. Monrovia, CA: MARC of World Vision, 1976.

Douglas, J. D., ed. *Let the Earth Hear His Voice.* Minneapolis, MN: World Wide, 1975.

Engel, James F. and Norton, H. Wilbert. *What's Gone Wrong With the Harvest?* Grand Rapids, MI: Zondervan, 1976.

Fife, Eric and Glasser, Arthur. *Missions in Crisis.* Downers Grove, IL: InterVarsity Press, 1961.

Glasser, Arthur; Heibert, Paul; Wagner, Peter; Winter, Ralph. *Crucial Dimensions in World Evangelization.* South Pasadena, CA: William Carey Library, 1976.

Goddard, Burton L. *The Encyclopedia of Modern Christian Missions.* Camden, NJ: Thomas Nelson & Sons, 1967.

Griffiths, Michael C. *Give Up Your Small Ambitions.* Chicago, IL: Moody Press, 1972.

Grubb, Sir Kenneth. *The Need for Non-Professional Missionaries.* London: World Dominion, January 1931.

Halverson, Richard. *How I Changed My Thinking about the Church.* Grand Rapids, MI: Zondervan, 1972.

Hefley, James & Marti. *Uncle Cam.* Waco, TX: Word, 1974.

Holland, H. B. T. *No Second Spring?* London: C.M.S., 1951.

Hyde, Douglas. *Dedication and Leadership: Learning From the Communists.* Notre Dame, IN: University of Notre Dame Press, 1966.

Johnston, P. J. *Operation World: A Handbook for World Intercession.* Bromley, Kent, England: STL Publications, 1978.

Kane, J. Herbert. *A Global View of Christian Missions.* Grand Rapids: Baker, 1971.

———. *Understanding Christian Missions.* Grand Rapids, MI: Baker, 1974.

———. *Winds of Change in Christian Mission.* Chicago, IL: Moody Press, 1973.

Kennedy, James. *Evangelism Explosion.* Wheaton, IL: Tyndale, 1977.

Kinnear, Angus I. *Against the Tide: The Story of Watchman Nee.* Eastbourne, Sussex, England: Victory Press, 1973; U.S. edition, Wheaton, IL: Tyndale House, 1978.

Kinnsler, Ross. *The Extension Movement in Theological Education.* South Pasadena, CA: William Carey Library, 1978.

Kraemer, Hendrik. *A Theology of the Laity.* Philadelphia: Westminster Press, 1958.

Krupp, Nate. *A World to Win.* Minneapolis, MN: Bethany Fellowship, 1966.

Lederer, W. J. and Burdick, E. *The Ugly American.* New York: Fawcett, 1963.

Lockerbie, D. Bruce. *Education of Missionaries' Children: The Neglected Dimension of World Mission.* Pasadena, CA: William Carey Library, 1975.

Mayer, Jenny de. *Adventures With God.* Toronto, Canada: Evangelical Publishers, 1942.

Merrell, James L. *They Live Their Faith.* St. Louis, MO: Bethany Press, 1966.

Mulholland, Kenneth. *Adventures in Training the Ministry.* Nutley, NJ: Presbyterian & Reformed Publishing Company, 1976.

Nash, Margaret. *Christians—World Citizens.* London: Edinburgh House, 1965.

Neill, Stephen. *A History of Christian Missions.* Middlesex, England: Penguin, 1977.

Neill, Stephen; Anderson, Gerald H; Goodwin, John. *Concise Dictionary of the Christian World Mission.* Nashville/New York: Abingdon Press, 1971.

Neill, S. C. *The Laymen in Christian History.* Philadelphia, PA: Westminster Press, 1963.

Nelson, Marlin A. and Chun, Chaeok. *Asian Mission Societies: New Resources for World Evangelization.* Monrovia, CA: World Vision, MARC, 1976.

Newman, Joseph. *People Helping People.* U.S. Volunteers in Action, U.S. News & World Report Books, Washington, DC, 1971.

Pennell, Theodore. *Among the Wild Tribes of the Afghan Frontier.* London: Seeley, 1909.

Perkins, Justin. *Missionary Life in Persia.* Boston, MA: American Tract Society, 1861.

Phelps, Cathy. *The Guide to Moving Overseas.* Box 236, Lamont, PA 16851: privately published, 1978.

Preheim, Marion K. *Overseas Service Manual.* Scottdale, PA: Herald Press, 1969.

Rees, Paul. *Nairobi to Berkley.* Monrovia, CA: World Vision, 1967.

Rosengrant, John. *Assignment: Overseas.* New York, NY: Thomas Y. Crowell, 1960.

Rowe, Jeanne A. *United Nations Workers: Their Jobs, Their Goals, Their Triumphs.* New York: Franklin Watts, 1970.

Sayre, Marcia. *Research for Mission Strategy in Iran.* Upper Darby, PA: BMMF, 1976.

Semands, John T. *Around the World for Christ.* Wilmore, KY: private publication, 1973.

————. *The Supreme Task of the Church.* Grand Rapids, MI: Eerdmans, 1964.

Soltau, T. Stanley. *Missions at the Crossroads.* Wheaton, IL: Van Kampen, 1954.

Stewart, John. *The Nestorian Missionary Enterprise: A Church on Fire.* Edinburgh, Scotland: Clarke, 1923.

Stott, John R. W. *Our Guilty Silence.* Downers Grove, IL: InterVarsity Press, 1970.

Strachan, R. Kenneth. *Evangelism In Depth.* Chicago: Moody Press, 1967.

————. *The Inescapable Calling.* Grand Rapids, MI: Eerdmans, 1968.

Taylor, Mrs. Howard. *Behind the Ranges, Fraser of Lisuland.* London: Lutterworth, 1944.

Thiessen, John. *A Survey of World Missions.* Downers Grove, IL: InterVarsity Press, 1956.

Tippett, A. R. *Bibliography For Cross-cultural Workers.* Pasadena, CA: William Carey Library, 1971.

Turner, Mrs. Solveig M. *International Encyclopedia of Higher Education.* Boston: Northeastern University, 1977.

Voelkel, Jack W. *Student Evangelism in a World of Revolution.* Grand Rapids: Zondervan, 1974.

Wagner, C. Peter. *Stop the World, I Want to Get On.* Glendale, CA: Gospel Light, 1974.

Warren, Max A. C. *Missions Under the Cross.* London: Edinburgh House, 1953.

Winfield, Louise. *Living Overseas.* Washington, DC: Public Affairs Press, 1962.

Wilson, J. Christy Jr. *One Hundred Afghan Persian Proverbs.* Kabul, Afghanistan: published privately, 1956.

Winter, Ralph. *Theological Education By Extension.* Pasadena, CA: William Carey, 1969.

Winter, Roberta H. *Once More Around Jericho.* Pasadena, CA: William Carey Library, 1978.

BIBLIOGRAPHY/ARTICLES

Bell, Bruce. "Where the Action Isn't," *Christianity Today,* Washington, DC, October 7, 1977, p. 29.

Butler, Phillip. "Missionaries: How to Bring Them In," *Advent Christian Missions,* November, 1977, pp. 6, 7.

Grubb, Sir Kenneth. "Laymen Abroad," *Frontier,* Vol. 4, No. 4, Winter, 1961, pp. 236, 237.

Grubbs, W. Eugene. "What Are Southern Baptist Laymen Doing Overseas?" *The Commission,* Richmond, VA, January, 1974, p. 5.

Hian, Chua Wee. "An IFES Overview: Past, Present and Future," *Branch,* Madison, WI, September 1, 1977, p. 3.

Hopewell, James F. "Training a Tent Making Ministry," *International Review of Missions,* 1966, pp. 333–339.

Iliff, Arthur D. "Missions on the Borders of Afghanistan," July, 1942, p. 4.

Kinsler, Ross. "Bases For Change in Theological Education," *Latin American Pulse,* August 1977.

Kling, August J. "Columbus—A Layman 'Christ-bearer' to Uncharted Isles," *The Presbyterian Layman,* October 1971, p. 4.

Kroeker, Wally. "They Witness While They Work," *Moody Monthly,* Vol. 75, No. 2, October 1974.

Kurtz, Robert. "The Lay-Worker as a New Type of Missionary," *The International Review of Missions,* July, 1953, Vol. 42, No. 167, p. 314.

Loeffler, Paul. "Laymen in World Mission," *International Review of Missions,* No. 53, 1964, pp. 297–308.

_____. "The Layman Abroad in the Mission of the Church," *International Missionary Council Research Pamphlets,* London: Edinburgh House Press, 1962.

MARC, Country Profiles, Monrovia, CA: World Vision.

_____. "Self-Supporting Missionaries: Problems & Opportunities," *Mission Handbook,* Section IV, Monrovia, CA: World Vision, October (1975) 1973.

Mattsson-Boze, Howard. "Self-Supporting Missionaries: Problems & Opportunities," IVCF, 1977.

McGavran, Donald. "The Genesis & Strategy of the Homogeneous Unit Principle," a paper delivered at the Lausanne Theology & Education Group Consultation on the Homogeneous Unit Principle, Fuller Theological Seminary, Pasadena, CA, May 31—June 2, 1977.

Niles, Preman. "Ministry of the Laity in Asia," *International Review of Missions,* *59,* 1970, pp. 162–172.

Parmer, S. L. "The Role of the European Expatriate in Asia," *International Review of Missions, 59,* 1970, pp. 450–460.

Roberts, David. "Laymen's Work in Europe," *Christian Century,* September 15, 1949, pp. 115–117.

Scott, Waldron. "The Student Missions Movement," an address given at the Association of Church Missions Committees in Wheaton, IL, 1977 (a tape).

Smeenge, Rev. Ronald C. "Meeting the Spiritual Needs of the U.S. Minority Overseas," *Evangelical Missions Quarterly,* Vol. 14, No. 2, April 1978, pp. 107–109, 128.

Ward, Ted. "Options for Overseas Service in World Evangelism," *Christ the Liberator,* 1971.

Wilson, J. Christy, Jr. "Witness While You Work Abroad," *Interlit,* Spring 1974.

Winter, Ralph. "The Grounds for a New Thrust in World Mission," *William Carey Library,* 1977, p. 2.

————. "Who are the Three Billion?," *Church Growth Bulletin,* Box 66, Santa Clara, CA 95050, Volume 13, No 6, July 1977, p. 144.

LIST OF ORGANIZATIONS AND ADDRESSES

In August, 1984, Overseas Counseling Service merged with CRISTA (the parent organization of Intercristo).

Now, there is an organization addressing the critical needs of tentmakers.

OCS provides the following services

1. Mobilization of tentmakers
2. Placement of tentmakers
3. Preparation of tentmakers
4. Nurturing of tentmakers
5. Networking of tentmakers
6. Research on tentmaking

For more information:

phone OCS (206) 546-7555

write OCS Box 33836, Seattle, WA 98133

1. Orientation Programs for Student Tentmakers Going Abroad
   Campus Crusade for Christ International (Agape Movement),
      Arrowhead Springs, San Bernardino, CA 92414. Ph. (714) 886-5224.
   Inter-Varsity, 233 Langdon, Madison, WI 53703. Ph. (608) 257-0263.
   Missionary Internship, P.O. Box 457, Farmington, MI 48024.
      Ph. (313) 474-9110.
   The Navigators, P.O. Box 1659, Colorado Springs, CO 80901.
      Ph. (303) 634-2861.
   Operation Mobilization, P.O. Box 148, Midland Park, NJ 07432.
      Ph. (201) 447-3715 (Canada: 646 Spadina Ave., Toronto, M5S 2H4.)
   Young Life Campaign, P.O. Box 520, Colorado Springs, CO 80901.
      Ph. (303) 598-5316.
   Youth for Christ International, P.O. Box 419, Wheaton, IL 60187.
      Ph. (312) 668-6600.
2. Tentmaking in Professional, Governmental, and Medical Capacities
   ACTION, 806 Connecticut Ave., N.W., Washington, DC 20525.
   Agency for International Development (USAID), Main State Bldg.,
      Washington, DC 20523.
   Christian Service Corps, 1509 Sixteenth St., N.W., Washington DC
      20036.

Inter Link, Box 832, Wheaton, IL 60187. Ph. (312) 665-7863.
MAP International, 327 Gundersen Dr., Carol Stream, IL 60187.
United Nations, Office of the Secretary-General, New York, NY 10017.
3. Tentmaking Literature and Periodicals
American Bible Society, 1865 Broadway, New York, NY 10023.
Christian Life, Gundersen Dr., Wheaton, IL 60187.
Christianity Today (subscription address), Box 354, Dover, NJ 07801.
The Church Around the World (Tyndale House Publishers),
   336 Gundersen Dr., Wheaton, IL 60187.
Church Growth Bulletin (Church Growth Book Club) Box 66,
   Santa Clara, CA 95050.
Eternity, 1716 Spruce St., Philadelphia, PA 19103.
Evangelical Missions Information Service (Evangelical Missions
   Quarterly), Box 794, Wheaton, IL 60187.
International Review of Mission (World Council of Churches),
   Room 1062, 475 Riverside Dr., New York, NY 10027.
Missiology, 1605 E. Elizabeth St., Pasadena, CA 91104.
Moody Monthly, (Moody Bible Institute), 820 N. La Salle St.,
   Chicago, IL 60610.
World Vision Magazine (Missions Advanced Research and
   Communications Center, Country Profiles), 919 W. Huntington Dr.,
   Monrovia, CA 91016.
4. Practical Information for Tentmakers
Guide to Moving Overseas (Cathy S. Phelps), Box 236, Lemont, PA
   16851.
Evangelical Foreign Mission Association (Fay Richardson),
   P.O. Box 5, Wheaton, IL 60187.
Mission Handbook (World Vision's MARC), Monrovia, CA.
5. Training for Future Tentmakers
Campus Crusade for Christ (Agape Movement), Arrowhead Springs,
   San Bernardino, CA 92414.
Christian Service Corps, 1509 Sixteenth St., N.W., Washington DC
20036.
Evangelical Foreign Missions Association, 1405 G Street, N.W.,
   Washington, DC 20005.
Gordon-Conwell Theological Seminary, South Hamilton, MA 01982,
   has a course in "Tentmaking Witness at Home and Abroad."
Institute in Basic Youth Conflicts, Box 1, Oak Brook, IL 60521.
Intercristo, Box 33487, Seattle, WA 98133.
Inter-Varsity Christian Fellowship (Urbana), 233 Langdon St.,
   Madison, WI 65703.
Missionary Internship, 36200 Freedom Road, Box 457, Farmington,
   MI 48024.
The Navigators, Box 1659, Colorado Springs, CO 80901.
Operation Mobilization, Box 184, Midland Park, NJ 07432.
W. Shabaz Associates, 16580 Eastland, Roseville, MI 48066.

U.S. Center for World Mission, 1605 East Elizabeth St.,
Pasadena, CA 91104, with its Institute of International Studies.
Youth with a Mission, Box 1099, Sunland, CA 91040.

6. Listings for Employment Abroad
   A Directory of American Firms Operating in Foreign Countries.
   Published by the World Trade Academy Press, Inc., 50 East 42nd
   Street, New York, NY.
   Foreign Employment Digest. P.O. Box 721, Peabody, MA 01961.
   Guide to Employment Abroad. Hill International Publications,
   P.O. Box 79, East Islip, Long Island, NY 11730.
   International Encyclopedia of Higher Education, ed. by Asa S. Knowles.
   (San Francisco, CA: Jossey-Boss, 1977), 10 volumes.
   Teaching Opportunities Overseas. Hill International Publications,
   P.O. Box 79, East Islip, Long Island, NY 11730.

7. Assistance in Placement of Tentmakers Abroad
   OCS, P.O. Box 33836, Seattle, WA 98133, Phone toll-free
   800-426-1343. (206) 546-7555 from AK, HI, WA and Canada.
   The Samuel Zwemer Institute (for Muslim countries only), P.O. Box
   365, Altadena, CA 91001. Ph. (213) 794-1121.
   W. Shabaz Associates, 16580 Eastland, Roseville, MI 48066.
   Ph. (313) 774-2300.

8. Assistance Regarding English-Speaking Churches Abroad
   International Fellowship of Christians, Ronald Smeenge, Director,
   P.O. Box 404, Grand Haven, MI 49417
   Program for Churchmen Overseas, John Collins, Director, NCCC,
   475 Riverside Drive, New York, NY 10027.

9. Agencies for Contacting International Students
   International Students Inc., Star Ranch, P.O. Box C, Colorado
   Springs, CO 80901. Ph. (303) 475-9500.
   International Student Ministry, Campus Crusade for Christ,
   Arrowhead Springs, San Bernardino, CA 92414. Ph. (714)
   886-5224.
   Inter-Varsity's Ministry with International Students, 233 Landgon,
   Madison, WI 53703. Ph. (608) 257-0263.

10. Agency for Studying or Teaching in Mainland China
    Committee on Scholarly Communication with the Peoples Republic
    of China, National Academy of Sciences, 2101 Constitution
    Avenue, Washington, D.C., 20418. Ph. (202) 393-8100.

11. Linguistic Training for Learning Languages
    Wycliffe Summer Institute of Linguistics offered at the Universities of
    North Dakota, Oklahoma, Washington (Seattle), and Texas
    (Arlington, Fall and Spring) as well as in Australia, Brazil, England
    Germany, Japan, and Mexico. Contact S.I.L., 7500 W. Camp
    Wisdom Road, Dallas, TX 75236; Toronto Institute of Linguistics,
    3425 Bayview Ave., Willowdale, ON, M2M 3S5, Canada.

12. Training in Teaching of English as a Second Language
    A one-year graduate school Master's program offered at the William Carey University, Center for World Mission, 1605 E. Elizabeth St., Pasadena, CA 91104. Ph. (213) 681-7959.